PRAISE FOR *HELP YOUR CHILD BUILD WEALTH*

"This is a wonderful book about stock market investing. I highly recommend it to readers of my syndicated financial column—for both young children and interested adults. Everything you need to know to get started and remain successful in stock market investing is in this book. And that's the savage truth!"

—**Terry Savage**, nationally syndicated financial columnist

"Readers of all ages will enjoy reading Mike Sincere's *Help Your Child Build Wealth*. Mike introduces his readers to the stock market by taking them down an easy-to-understand path that explains why it's important to invest in the market, how to open a stock brokerage account, how to build wealth with index funds, and how to profit from stocks. He explains key strategies for investing, as well as warning of risks to avoid. Mike is a best-selling author, trader, and educator, and he is a top-notch guide to lead readers of all ages (and you!) through the halls of the stock market."

—**Toni Turner**, author of *A Beginner's Guide to Day Trading Online*, Second Edition

"Michael Sincere's latest book, *Help Your Child Build Wealth*, is his best book yet as it extends investor education to the full spectrum of the population, meaning it trickles down to teens and tweens. This book is just the kind of gentle, pragmatic approach that parents need to connect with their children to give them a head start on taking control of their financial future."

—**Jeffrey Bierman**, CMT, professor of finance, Loyola University Chicago Quinlan School of Business; founder and chief market strategist, TheQuantGuy.com

T0307721

HELP YOUR CHILD BUILD WEALTH

HELP YOUR CHILD BUILD WEALTH

A PARENT'S GUIDE TO TEACHING CHILDREN TO BE SUCCESSFUL INVESTORS

MICHAEL SINCERE

WILEY

Library of Congress Cataloging-in-Publication Data

Names: Sincere, Michael, author. | John Wiley & Sons, publisher.
Title: Help your child build wealth : a parent's guide to teaching children
  to be successful investors / Michael Sincere.
Description: Hoboken, New Jersey : Wiley, [2025] | Includes index.
Identifiers: LCCN 2024021651 (print) | LCCN 2024021652 (ebook) | ISBN
  9781394257232 (paperback) | ISBN 9781394257249 (adobe pdf) | ISBN
  9781394257256 (epub)
Subjects: LCSH: Investments—Study and teaching. | Index mutual
  funds—Study and teaching. | Children—Finance, Personal.
Classification: LCC HG4514 .S56 2025 (print) | LCC HG4514 (ebook) | DDC
  332.6083—dc23/eng/20240628
LC record available at https://lccn.loc.gov/2024021651
LC ebook record available at https://lccn.loc.gov/2024021652

Cover Design: Jon Boylan
Cover Image: © Kabardins photo/Shutterstock
SKY10086355_100324

To my wonderful mother and father,
and also Chip, Chili,
and Lizzie

CONTENTS

CONTENTS

INTRODUCTION

T hank you for buying my book. I wrote this book for parents and
their children, or relatives, or for anyone else who wants to use the
stock market to build wealth. Teenagers who are interested in the
market can read this book on their own.

I did my best to make this one of the most helpful books about
investing you will ever read. If you believe that investing in the market
is complicated or time-consuming, I hope to surprise you. I wanted my
book to be a fast, enjoyable, and easy read. I teach only the most
important ideas—what you and your child (or children) need to know
right now.

Believe it or not, making money in the stock market is not that hard, as
long as you have a strategy (i.e., an investment plan) and follow a few rules.
Even more amazing, you and your child can beat the pros who analyze the
markets for a living on Wall Street (where the New York Stock Exchange
is located).

According to statistics, your child can beat more than 90% of the Wall
Street pros. Maybe you think this isn't possible or that I am making this up.
Nope. Anyone in the financial world knows that 90% of the pros fail to beat
the S&P 500 index each year. This fact is not a secret, but it's not information
the experts like to share.

What is the S&P 500 index? To learn more about this valuable financial product, keep reading. I'll show you exactly what you need to do to beat 90% of the Wall Street pros, and also help your child generate wealth.

Before you or your child can expect to outperform the experts, however, you must know more about the stock market.

WHAT YOU AND YOUR CHILD WILL LEARN

By the time you have read all or even part of this book, you will learn about the following subjects. (Don't worry if you don't understand everything on this list, because it will be explained later.)

- Begin by opening a stock brokerage account for yourself. By having your own investment account, it's easier to explain it to your children. Later, you can open an account for them.
- Invest at least $20 or $25 into an S&P 500 index fund, an investment that matches the performance of the S&P 500 index. In this book, you are going to learn everything you need to know about index funds, one of the smartest financial products ever created. Part I is all about investing in index funds.
- Invest a set amount of money each month into the same index fund, a strategy called *dollar cost averaging*.
- Hold the index fund indefinitely.
- When you've gained more experience as an investor, you may decide to buy individual stocks. Choose the right one and you can make good money. Investing in stocks is explained in Part II.

SHOULD YOUR CHILD INVEST IN THE STOCK MARKET?

Your child may ask why they should invest their money in the market. The answer is simple: tell them that the stock market is one of the greatest wealth-building systems ever created. It is how many people got rich in the past and will continue to do so in the future. The good news is you can get started with a small amount of money.

Since the US stock market was created in New York in 1792, the market has moved much, much higher. Here is a fact: the S&P index has an average yearly return of about 10.26% from 1957 to 2024 (https://bit .ly/3RtDQ9Q).

Depending on other factors (i.e., dividends and inflation), some analysts claimed that the actual yearly return is closer to 15%, while others caution that a return of approximately 7% is more reasonable.

Most important, by following the basic investing strategies introduced in this book, your child can be millionaires well before they are ready to retire. Many people made a lot of money investing in index funds, and your child can do the same.

Fact: If someone had invested $100 in the S&P 500 index in 1928 (before the 1929 stock market crash), that $100 would be worth more than $700,000 in 2024. In comparison, investing that same $100 in a 10-year Treasury (i.e., cash) in 1928 would be worth a little more than $8,500 (https://bit.ly/3XGIOUX).

Fact: A $1,000 investment in the S&P 500 in 2014 would be worth $3,300 in 2024 for an impressive average annual return of 12.68%. A $5,000 investment in 2014 would have returned $16,498 in 2024. A $10,000 investment would have grown to $32,997 in 2024 (https://bit.ly/3VrJmLo).

Money provides financial security. With the right investments, your child (or relatives) can buy what they need, travel, and enjoy the quality of life that only money can bring. I'm not saying that money is all-important, but it does make life easier. As your child goes through life, they will feel confident knowing they can handle most financial emergencies (and without relying on credit cards).

In fact, financial security is one of the best gifts you can give your child. They can achieve this goal by using some simple investment strategies. The idea is to build wealth over a lifetime so they don't have to worry about their next paycheck or paying for a medical emergency.

Some people spend their money on the lottery, hoping for a miracle. Your route will take longer but the odds of success are thousands of times greater. Fortunately, your child can have a comfortable life without waiting for a miracle.

Your child will discover that over time, stock market investing is the easiest, and one of the most dependable ways, for generating wealth. They will learn to set aside some money each month to buy shares of an index fund. Growth begins slowly, but a pot of cash could be waiting for them when they are older (as long as they follow a few rules).

Your child has a fantastic opportunity to become wealthy. Why? Because time is on their side. In fact, the earlier they start investing, the more money they can make. When you ask many older folks if they have any regrets about their finances, many say they wish they had started investing sooner. Don't make that mistake: teach your child how to invest in the stock market now. This gives them a chance to have a financially comfortable life.

The good news is you already took the first step: you bought this book. I'll do my best to make you happy with that decision.

As you keep reading, you'll find that it's not difficult to make money in the stock market. The hard part is having the *patience* and *discipline* to follow the strategies and obey the rules. If your children can do that, they can continue to build wealth for their entire lives.

Some of you may think that you need a lot of money to make money in the market. Sure, it helps, but it is not true. All you need to get started is a few dollars (or other currency).

The goal is to get into the habit of investing, even if it is a small sum. You can invest as little or as much money as you want. Later, as your children grow older and their income increases, they should be able to invest even more of their own money.

As you may have guessed, this is not a get-rich-quick book. The strategies in here are for long-term investors. The plan is to teach you and your child how to use money to make more money.

On the other hand, I know that for some children, the stock market is about as exciting as learning geometry or trigonometry. If that sounds like your child, be patient. One day, after they see how much money is in their account, their attitude is likely to change.

Right now, my goal is to teach you what you need to know about the stock market so that it is understandable, and hopefully, rewarding. Then you can pass that knowledge onto your children (or other relatives).

Note: If you are a teacher interested in teaching your students about the stock market, my book should meet your needs, no matter their age. This information can be adjusted to any grade level.

Speaking of teaching, it's unfortunate that most teachers aren't given much time to introduce their students to investing or money management. Ideally, children should learn about saving money early in life. Instead, most learn how to spend (usually with credit cards), but not how to invest. Perhaps that's why so many people get into financial difficulties later in life.

HOW TO PARTICIPATE IN THE STOCK MARKET

There are two main ways to participate in the stock market. The preferred way is to be an *investor*, which means buying and holding index funds and other financial products for long time periods—which could be for years. This has been a proven method for generating wealth.

The other choice is to be a *trader*, which means buying and selling stocks over a very short time period. It could be a day, week, or a couple of months. Trading is a risky method best left to the professionals who do it for a living. Why? Because being a successful trader takes a tremendous amount of skill and discipline. It's extremely difficult for anyone to predict where stock prices are headed in the next few minutes, days, or months.

For most people, and especially your children, the *only* way to be in the market is as an investor. This is because investing is far less risky. Also, it's easier to make money, you buy but rarely sell, and it doesn't take a lot of time to learn.

IS INVESTING COMPLICATED?

Some people stay away from investing because they believe it is too difficult to learn. Others believe they need a lot of money to get started.

Fortunately, I cut through all of the confusion and show that investing is not that hard.

I'm not the first to create the strategies included in this book but because of my background as a teacher, I'm one of the few who can make it understandable.

To answer the question, is investing complicated?: investing is not complicated. Many people try to make it seem harder than it is. In reality, the challenge is sticking to the simple strategies that you'll learn about in this book.

LET'S BEGIN

And now, let's begin learning how to use the stock market to enrich yourself and your child. By the time you get to the end of the book, you may think differently about investing, and that is good. Although some folks chase after the next hot stock or new investment idea, you and your child will patiently invest a set amount of money each month into index funds while slowly watching your profits grow. It can't get any better than that!

I hope that reading this book will help to motivate you to discuss investing with your child. Discussing money and personal finance early in life will benefit them. Perhaps this book will help start that conversation. I also made a list of understandable definitions that should be useful (see the Glossary).

Another goal is to help your children have a healthy relationship with money. They should learn that money is important but it's not the most important thing in life (some people may disagree!). Teaching your children how to control money, rather than letting money control them, will reduce future heartache.

PART I

BUILD WEALTH WITH INDEX FUNDS

A re you ready to go on a profitable journey? In Part I, you'll learn about building wealth with *index funds*, one of the most ingenious investment products in history.

It's not only index funds, but I also write about *mutual funds* and *exchange-traded funds* (*ETFs*). There is a lot of information in Part I, but I did my best to make it interesting as well as educational. You will definitely learn a lot.

> Note: There are five main types of investments: cash, stocks, real estate, bonds, and alternative investments such as digital currencies (Bitcoin), collectables (art), and gold. As you will learn, the primary focus is on index funds, but I'll discuss other investments in later chapters.

CHAPTER ONE

INVESTING 101

I n this chapter, I introduce you to the stock market and teach you a few basic vocabulary words. I'll focus only on the most important strategies and ideas. Although this part is about index funds, it's important to have a basic understanding of the stock market and stocks.

WHAT IS
THE STOCK MARKET?

The stock market is a place where buyers and sellers trade stocks, index funds, bonds, and other financial products. Put another way, the stock market is similar to being at a street market. However, instead of buying and selling stuff at a market, you buy and sell stocks, which represents part ownership in a corporation.

Put another way, a *stock* represents *shares* in a corporation such as Disney, Apple, Mattel, or Nike. When buying *shares* of stock in a corporation, the goal is to *share* in the success (or failure) of that corporation.

If your child is old enough to understand, with your help, you can ask them if they want to buy shares of Disney stock (or choose stock in another company they know well). After you buy the stock for them (which you will learn to do in Part II), explain they are now part owner of Disney (in this example).

If Disney does well and makes a profit, then the Disney stock you bought will go up in price—and you make money. However, if Disney does poorly and earnings drop, then the Disney stock you bought declines, and you lose money.

Why does a stock price go higher or lower? When a lot of people buy stock in the company, then the stock price rises. When a lot of people sell stock in the company, then the stock price falls. Investors and traders constantly buy and sell stock when the stock market is open. The more buyers, the higher the stock price goes. The more sellers, the lower the stock price goes.

In summary, when you invest in stocks, you are hoping that the company will be profitable and that the stock moves higher. You want the stock price to be higher than when you bought it. If you choose winning stocks, you will make money. If you choose losing stocks, you will lose money. My goal is to help you find the winners. It's that simple.

However, if buying shares of stock sounds complicated, don't worry. As you will learn, to make money in the stock market, you can buy individual stocks if you want to. As I discussed previously, an easier way to build wealth is by buying an index fund. Buying an index is not complicated, the math is basic, and as you will learn later, those who invest in indexes outperform nearly all professional money managers every year.

The following is a brief introduction to indexes, but you will learn much more about them in Chapter 3.

INDEXES: THE DOW, S&P 500, AND NASDAQ 100

When I refer to the stock market, I am really talking about investing in individual companies such as Disney, Nike, and Amazon. However, instead of buying any of these stocks, you can also buy market *indexes*.

An index is simply a basket of stocks grouped together into a *portfolio*. For example, the most well-known index in the world is the Dow Jones Industrial Average (DJIA). This index, affectionally known as *the Dow*, consists of 30 large, well-known "industrial" US companies.

Each day, the financial media (online, print, and television) broadcast how "the market" is doing, and that usually means the Dow. "The Dow is up 400 *points*," you may read or hear during the day. If the Dow is higher by over 400 *points* in one day, that is a good day for investors.

> Note: When the market or a stock goes higher or lower, Wall Street uses the word *point* to describe the price change.

The second most popular index is the S&P 500 (Standard & Poor's 500 Index). This closely followed index consists of 500 of the largest US corporations. It is also the index that most market professionals watch. Guess what? All of the stocks that I mentioned previously, including Disney, Nike, Amazon, and hundreds more, are in the S&P 500. As you will learn later, it's a lot easier to buy one index that includes all of these stocks.

Finally, the third most popular index is the Nasdaq-100, which consists of 100 of the largest, most actively traded companies listed on the Nasdaq stock exchange.

Here's the important part: although there are thousands of indexes, the index we are most interested in is the S&P 500. That is the index professional managers want to beat, and the index that I encourage you and your child to buy.

Truthfully, I'm getting a little ahead of myself as we will discuss the S&P 500 in greater detail in Chapter 3. The most important thing to remember is that there are individual stocks and there are indexes (which represent groups of stocks). I'll show you how to invest in both. Owning these investments is the key to building wealth over the long term.

THE RISKS

It is my responsibility as an author to alert you to the risks that await you when you enter the stock market. I wish I could say that everyone who invests makes money, but that's not true. Some people lose money.

Perhaps some of you are worried about this. Yes, there is a chance you may lose money if the entire market goes down. When you invest in the stock market, that can happen.

Fortunately, I'll tell you exactly what to do when there is a large stock market decline. I also offer ideas of what to buy so that you won't lose money over a long time period (however, it's always possible to lose in the short term). Even better, I'll show you a strategy that is easy to use and understand, and has worked for decades.

Do you want to know what one of the biggest risks is? It's not investing at all. If you don't invest in the financial markets, you and your child will miss out on a fantastic opportunity to build future wealth for yourselves. Although there is always some risk, investing in the stock market is still one of the best ways to have a financially comfortable life.

WHY SOME PEOPLE DON'T INVEST

Some people don't invest in the stock market because they are afraid. Perhaps they heard scary stories of people who lost money after buying a terrible stock. Other people think the stock market is too confusing.

Some people believe that the stock market is a gambling casino. It's true there are financial strategies that make investing similar to a casino. Fortunately, we will not be using those strategies. Instead, you will learn to be in the stock market without taking extreme risks (I didn't say there were no risks, but there will be *less* risk).

The only way to avoid any financial risk is by putting your money into a *savings account* or *money market account.* If you take this route, after 70 years, your child's money will still be there, but I guarantee it will be worth a lot less because of *inflation.*

However, if you put that same money into the stock market, you should be pleased with the results.

Note: Putting money into a savings account won't generate wealth, but it's a good place to start teaching young children about investing. You can also use the savings account to teach children how to store money for emergencies.

To help motivate your child to deposit more cash into a savings account (and later in an investment account), you may want to offer to match a portion of their contributions. For example, if your child saves $10, agree to a 50% match, or $5. You can also look for ways to add money to the savings account (such as a birthday gift).

After opening a savings account, you can open a brokerage account. Many children have their own savings account, but only a few have an investment account. With your help, your child will move from being just a saver to being an investor.

After you've read this book, they can join this elite group.

WHY IT'S OKAY IF THE MARKET GOES DOWN

It doesn't matter if the market goes higher or lower as long as you participate. For example, if you are reading this book during a *correction* (the market has fallen by more than 10% in a few days) or a *bear market* (the market has fallen by more than 20% in a short time period), you are lucky. This is a good time to invest.

Why? It means that you and your child can buy stocks when they are on sale. The stock market is a marketplace, and the lower the prices, the better the deal. If your child uses the *indexing strategy* I introduce in Chapter 2, they should almost certainly do well later in life.

Although other people tend to panic when the market falls, you should be teaching your child to see it as a buying opportunity. "Hey, everyone, the market is on sale! It's time to invest more money into the stock market." Guess what? That is the opposite of what most people do!

PAY YOURSELF FIRST

I also hope you show your children how to pay themselves first. That means learning to set aside a part of their income for investing. As they get older, it is hoped that they pay themselves first before they pay their bills. One day, when they work for a company or themselves, they can automatically take part of their paycheck to invest in the stock market.

Note: When your child gets a job, paying themself first will be easier if the company they work for has a *401(k) plan*. This excellent program enables employees to invest part of their salary into an index fund, or an investment of their choice. The 401(k) is not subject to taxes until the money is withdrawn. Typically, the employer contributes to the plan by matching up to a certain percentage of the paycheck. This is what gives older children and adults a savings boost. If your child has a job and can participate in a 401(k) plan, by all means encourage them to do so. See a tax or finance professional for any tax-related questions about this plan.

CONCLUSION

Now that you have an overview of the stock market, it's time to get to work. In the next chapter, I discuss how to open a brokerage account for yourself and your child. If you've never opened a brokerage account before, don't be concerned. Once the account is open, it's easy to invest.

Note: While reading this book, if you are stuck on a vocabulary word or strategy, a great stock market resource is Investopedia (www.investopedia.com). You can also look in the glossary of this book for a list of understandable definitions.

CHAPTER TWO

THE BROKERAGE ACCOUNT

The most difficult part for many parents is taking that first step and opening the brokerage account. Once the account is open, the learning begins. Most important, understanding the stock market, finances, and how to manage money is critical for your child's financial education.

It doesn't matter if the market moves up or down, how young or old your child is, or how little or how much money you have: start by opening a brokerage account. This is a call to action: do it soon.

The goal is to open the account and begin by investing each month. After a while, it will become as routine as paying a bill, taking out the garbage, or washing the dishes. Hopefully, you will raise a financially savvy child.

The sooner you and your child start investing, the better the chances they will be financially secure one day. This is not a sprint but a long-distance marathon.

You can open a brokerage account by visiting the firm's website, opening an app (discussed later), or visiting the firm's office (if they have one). Let's find out more about brokerage firms.

STOCK BROKERAGE FIRMS

A brokerage is a company that is licensed to buy and sell stocks and other financial products on behalf of its clients (such as you). Placing orders (buying and selling) may be done with an online brokerage firm where you can trade over the internet, or with a firm that has real people taking orders. Many brokers allow both methods.

After your brokerage account is open (which is as easy as opening a checking or savings account), I'll show you which financial products to buy.

You can choose any brokerage firm that you want (and there are hundreds), but I recommend choosing one with an excellent reputation, that's open at least 12 hours a day for questions or chat, and has low fees and commissions, if any.

Because all brokerage firms have a website, most allow buying or selling using your computer, phone, or tablet. Brokerage firms offer educational resources and information about investing strategies. This is an excellent place to further your education.

Before signing with a broker, call, email, or chat with a representative to see how quickly they respond to questions. If satisfied with their service, then apply online or with an app. You can also visit the firm if they have a brick-and-mortar building.

If you choose the right broker, it's likely you and your child will be customers for a long time. Nevertheless, if dissatisfied with their service for any reason, it's easy to cancel the account and move it elsewhere.

THE BROKERAGE ACCOUNT

Although there are several ways to manage your brokerage account, the reason you bought this book and the recommended method is to do it yourself. You choose the financial products to buy or sell and manage the account on your own with a brokerage firm. After reading this book, most of you will choose this method.

> Note: The other two methods are using a *robo-advisor* (discussed in Chapter 12), or paying a percentage of your investment to a stockbroker (i.e., professional money manager) to create a personalized portfolio. For large accounts, a money manager will oversee the account, make buy and sell decisions on your behalf, and periodically discuss your investments.

TOP STOCK BROKERAGE FIRMS

Following are three excellent brokerage firms for both beginners and experienced investors who manage their own accounts. These firms have no minimum investment requirements and no commissions. There are hundreds of other excellent brokerage firms that want your business, so do your research before choosing.

- **Charles Schwab & Company**
  Schwab is accessible through their investment app, online, or by visiting their brick-and-mortar office. They have excellent customer service with knowledgeable representatives and 24/7 phone and chat support. They also provide a huge selection of financial

products, extensive research, low fees, and hundreds of branches around the country.

- **Fidelity**

  You can access Fidelity via their investment app, online, or visit one of their brick-and-mortar brokerage firms. They have a huge selection of financial products, especially mutual funds, knowledgeable representatives, 24/7 phone and chat support, low fees, excellent research, and hundreds of branches around the country.

- **Vanguard**

  Vanguard is suitable for buy-and-hold investors, especially those who buy mutual funds and index funds. They are known for their no-transaction-fee mutual funds and ETFs, and for being the first to offer index funds (although some funds require a $3,000 minimum investment). They have 12-hour phone support and basic educational resources. Their trading platform is aimed at long-term investors, not active traders. You can reach Vanguard online or with an app. They do not have brick-and-mortar offices.

As your children get older, they may have their own ideas about which brokerage firm to choose. Sure, let them choose the brokerage they want, as long as the firm has a good reputation. Evaluate the brokerage using the following sources.

Hint: If you are interested in looking at other brokerage firms, go to any search engine and type "rank online brokerage firms" followed by the current year. This will bring up a list of articles from independent sources such as *Forbes*, *Barron's*, MarketWatch, *Kiplinger*, *USA Today*, NerdWallet, and Bankrate, which should help with your decision.

OPENING A BROKERAGE ACCOUNT

Once again, choose a brokerage firm that meets your needs. Then enroll online, with an app, or at the broker's office (if they have one). If you have questions, feel free to call for help.

If your child or relative is over 18 years old, they may want to open a brokerage account on their own. This should be encouraged. If your child is under 18 years old, you may open a *custodial account* (explained in Chapter 6) or teach them how to invest using your own brokerage account.

When first signing onto a brokerage website, you'll be asked to create a User ID and password. Next, fill out the form beginning with your Social Security number and date of birth.

You will be asked basic questions about your investment experience, along with your financial objectives, the products you want to own, and the risk you are willing to accept (from low to high). Don't worry too much about the answers to the questionnaire. The answers are used only for informational purposes. (After reading this book, you will have no problem with the answers.)

One question is whether you want to open a *margin* account. Margin enables a customer to borrow money from the broker to buy more shares. If you are a beginner, I recommend *not* applying for margin. Margin has caused problems for investors who don't understand how easy it is to lose more money than they have. You can always add margin later if you wish. (Fortunately, buying and holding an index fund does not require a margin account.)

FUNDING THE ACCOUNT

When the questionnaire is finished, you will be asked how you will "fund" the account (i.e., deposit cash that can be used to buy an index fund, stocks,

23

or other investments). You don't have to transfer money right away, but eventually you should set up the account so you can move money from your bank account to the brokerage firm.

Typically, the transferred money is put into a money market account until you are ready to buy something. It's not a problem if you don't want to invest money right now. You can open the account at most brokerages with no minimum investment.

All of the products you can buy or sell are listed in a drop-down menu on the website. When you have time, become familiar with the screens. For now, all you need to know is the name or symbol of the index fund or stock you want to buy. Every financial product has a symbol.

Example: If you wanted to buy stock in Amazon, the symbol is AMZN. If you wanted to buy shares of stock in Disney, the symbol is DIS. If you wanted to invest in the S&P 500 index, you can buy the SPDR *S&P 500 ETF*, whose symbol is SPY. It's easy to find the symbol for any stock, index, mutual fund, or ETF you want to buy.

HOW TO BUY AN INDEX FUND (OR STOCK)

In reality, one of the easiest things to do on the brokerage website is buying or selling an index fund (or stock). Brokerage firms have spent millions of dollars to make this an enjoyable experience. Here's a brief explanation how to buy an index or stock during normal market hours, Monday through Friday.

After entering the correct stock or index symbol on the screen, enter the size of your investment or how many *shares* you want to buy. It can be as little or as much as you want (but a minimum of 1 share). After that, press the BUY button. The computer calculates how much it will cost to buy the index fund or stock.

If done correctly, the purchase will be made immediately.

Yes, it's that easy. (If you want more detailed instructions, at the beginning of Chapter 10, I list all the steps needed to buy a stock or index fund.)

Buying your first index fund can be thrilling. Your child can immediately view the total value of the account. For many children, it's fun to watch the price move higher or lower each day (especially as it moves higher).

Teach your child to read the brokerage statement (either online or in print), the value of the account, and the current price of the index fund. For some children, looking at the profit and loss screen on their computer will motivate them to put even more money into their brokerage account. They can always invest extra money when it comes their way through gifts, work, or an allowance.

> Hint: Explain to your child that no matter how high or low the index fund goes, it should not be sold.

THE INVESTMENT GAME

You can also make investing into a game, what I call The Investment Game. Challenge your child to put more money into the account, and use a dollar figure when they are old enough to understand. For example, you can say, "Let's try to put $20 into the account this month."

As long as the account is growing and making money, the game is fun. Sometimes, there will be bad months and it may not be as fun, and your child may lose interest. Do what you can to keep them involved.

The good news: based on more than 200 years of stock market returns, the market has always come back, even after some awful years. That's when your children should be amazed that the investment they made when they were younger is worth a lot more than it cost. That's when The Investment Game is fun again.

> Note: For adults, investing in the stock market should not be used as entertainment. In fact, it's serious business. However, to motivate children, it is appropriate to make investing into a fun game with a goal to increase profits.

Now that you have an idea of how to open a brokerage account, you need to go out and do it. To help your child have a lifetime of financial security, it is important to begin. Opening a brokerage account is the first step.

Investment Apps

One of the most popular ways to interact with your broker is to use a mobile application, or app. Let's discuss these in more detail.

The investing world has changed a lot over the last couple of years. Now, many children (and their parents) open an account, get stock ideas, and invest in the market using apps. Investing apps are here to stay, and new ones are being written all the time. The key is to find the specific apps that meet your needs.

Apps are excellent tools that track stocks, manage a portfolio, save money, perform research, and get news. They also display stock quotes and charts, and help with buy, sell, and hold decisions.

Apps can be installed on computers (desktop apps), tablets, or on smartphones (mobile apps). More than likely, your children are primarily using mobile apps. You can search for apps for both Apple (Apple Store) and Android devices (Google Play).

Using an app to set up your brokerage account is the same as setting it up online. You must provide personal information such as your name, address, and Social Security number.

Although mobile apps are gaining in popularity, especially with younger investors, desktop apps remain more popular with professional traders and most adults. Brokerages have solved this problem by creating apps for both desktop and mobile devices.

To find a list of the top investment apps, type "rank top investing apps" followed by the current year into a search engine. A current list of apps from independent sources will be displayed.

CONCLUSION

After opening a brokerage account, it's time to make money. Although there are thousands of choices of what financial products to buy, in Chapter 3, I'll tell you some of the best to consider.

CHAPTER THREE

INVEST IN INDEX FUNDS

I n this chapter, you will learn that a very simple and one of the most profitable strategies is investing in an *index fund*. Although there are no guarantees this product will make you wealthy, the odds of success over the longer term are on your side.

As mentioned in the Introduction, if your child uses the simple indexing strategy, they will beat more than 90% of professional fund managers. The longer they hold onto their index fund, the better. By being an "indexer," you can help your child build wealth.

THE S&P 500 INDEX FUND

What exactly is an index fund? It is a simply a portfolio (i.e., basket) of stocks that matches the overall performance of the entire market, or a certain market sector. The index that we are most interested in is the S&P 500, which is also the most popular index in the world.

As you may have guessed, there are 500 stocks in the index. Basically, the S&P 500 tries to copy or mimic the performance of the 500 stocks in the S&P 500. If you had tried to build your own stock portfolio with these stocks, it would be too expensive.

When you own shares in an index fund such as the S&P 500, instead of trying to beat the S&P 500, you simply follow along. That is a good thing. Therefore, when the S&P 500 rallies by 4% today, then the S&P 500 index fund that you own increases by 4%.

By buying an index fund, you get to go along for the ride with one simple "buy" transaction. Owning shares of an index has been one of the most efficient ways to participate in the stock market.

The 500 stocks in the index are some of the most popular and successful companies in the world. They are also the largest (as measured by *market capitalization*). For example, think of a company where you shop or use their products. Perhaps you thought of Amazon, Apple, Google, Microsoft, Netflix, Disney, Home Depot, Lowe's, Walmart, Costco, to name a few. All of these companies are in the S&P 500 index.

Even more important, when you invest in the S&P 500, you are betting that the US stock market will continue to move higher over time. History has shown that it's a mistake to bet against the future of American business. That's why it makes sense to invest in the S&P 500, which reflects the financial strength of the US. (If you live in another country, you can invest in an index fund that is tied to your country's stock market.)

When the market is open, the 500 stocks in the index have a price change, sometimes higher, sometimes lower. In the short term, the index moves around a lot, sometimes with price changes as much as 1% or 2%. In the long term, the index price has generally risen, which is why investing in the index itself has been such a winning strategy. (Caveat: There are no guarantees it will go up every year.)

You may wonder why everyone isn't using the indexing strategy. The answer is that millions of people are—but not everyone.

Some investors have their own ideas of which stocks they want to own. Many people want to beat the stock market. With indexing, you simply match the stock market, and try not to beat it. Not everyone is a fan of that strategy.

CAN YOU DO BETTER THAN THE STOCK MARKET?

If you are a person who wants to do better than the stock market itself, you may not like indexing. For example, if you want to outdo the indexes (i.e., outperform them), turn to Part II where I discuss buying individual stocks. Nevertheless, I recommend indexing for most investors.

If you choose a winning stock, and there are many out there, you can outperform index funds. However, if you pick your own stocks, you must do your own research to find winners, which is not easy for most people.

However, if you want a less-risky strategy with a good chance to make excellent returns, you should consider buying index funds.

INTRODUCING INDEX FUNDS

Index funds were created by the late John Bogle in the 1950s when he was in college. Bogle believed that the best way for most investors to own common stocks is through an index fund that charges low fees.

After college, he founded the successful brokerage company Vanguard, which is devoted to index funds. At that time, the idea of not beating but matching the S&P 500 seemed ridiculous.

Bogle had the last laugh as the indexing strategy not only became wildly popular but also has worked over long time periods. Indexing is still one of the best ways to participate in the stock market but with reduced risk (but not zero risk).

There are a lot of interesting facts about index funds. First, there is no active manager deciding which stocks to buy or sell. With an index fund, the fund manager simply buys the 500 stocks in the index (using the money you and everyone else invested).

Because there is no active manager, index fund expenses are low, saving money for investors. That means you are not paying sales charges, advertising costs, and special fees that some funds charge for having a manager.

Because index funds were designed to match the stock market, an index fund obviously does great when the market is moving higher, and does poorly when the market is moving lower. Fortunately, the stock market has generally gone up over nearly every 10-year period, which is why index funds have done so well over the long term.

DIVERSIFICATION

Which stocks in the S&P 500 are going to outperform next year? The answer is, no one knows. Because the fund owns a part of each stock in the S&P 500, your investment is *diversified*, another way of reducing risk. To use an analogy, you are not putting all of your eggs in one basket. You are not trying to pick which stocks will be winners. Instead, you are placing a bet on all 500 stocks in the fund.

Diversification is one of the key goals of investors who don't like risks, another reason why it makes sense to buy an index fund. In fact, index proponents like to say they are getting "instant diversification," and they're right.

However, diversification limits your gains. For example, let's say that Apple's stock price increased by 5% one day. Because Apple is in the

S&P 500 index, although 5% is a spectacular one-day gain, other stocks in the index may not have done as well, which brings the total gain lower.

In other words, instead of the 5% you wanted to make that day, you may only have made 1% or 2%. Therefore, diversification works both ways: it protects you in case of a disaster but it also curbs how much you can make.

NO ONE DOES IT BETTER

I was fortunate to have learned about the indexing strategy from the man who created it, John Bogle. The strategy is easy to use, and anyone can succeed by following it.

I spent years writing about and studying investment strategies. Of all of the strategies I used, and I tried most of them, indexing is one of the best. Indexing enabled me and others to make a lot of money.

HOW AN INDEX FUND QUIETLY CREATES WEALTH

There are many ways your index fund makes money behind the scenes. To be specific, an index fund earns *dividends* and *compound interest*.

Dividends

Index funds pay quarterly *dividends* to their *shareholders* (investors who own the fund). For example, if you own an S&P 500 index fund, many of the stocks in the fund pay dividends, which are then automatically distributed to you. You have a choice: you can reinvest the money into your account to buy more shares, or you can take the cash. Suggestion: Reinvest all dividends.

That's one of the exciting things about owning an index fund (or a stock that pays dividends). You and your child make money consistently, what financial folks call an *income stream*. That's not all: by owning an index fund that pays dividends, it also leads to another profitable experience: compounding.

Compounding: The Eighth Wonder of the World

Another way that index funds generate extra money is through a fascinating financial phenomenon called *compounding*. Simply put, compounding means that investors earn extra money on the money they already invested.

To be specific, *compound interest* is the interest on both the original investment and on the new shares that were purchased with that interest. While you are at work or school, the boring index fund is compounding your profits to make extra profits.

For compounding to work, the earnings from an investment, including capital gains, interest, and dividends, must be returned to your account (i.e., reinvested).

I'll spare you the math behind compounding, but it's an eye-opener. Albert Einstein once said that compound interest is the "eighth wonder of the world." "He who understands it," he said, "earns it. He who doesn't, pays it."

John Bogle said that compounding was "the greatest mathematical discovery of all time for the investor seeking maximum reward."

When you buy and hold an index fund, you can watch the mathematical miracle of compounding help make you wealthy. As I said, the earlier your child starts investing, the more money they can earn.

Compound interest also works in reverse. In addition to charging obscenely high interest rates, credit card companies get rich when customers only pay the minimum amount due. It may take 10 or 20 years for customers to pay back the debt. It's the power of compound interest that keeps customers in debt for decades.

> Note: If you ever get into debt with a credit card, try to pay that debt back as quickly as possible. If you only pay the minimum, you'll be stuck in a debt hole for a long time (thanks to compound interest).

Is there anything bad about earning money from compounding? The answer is no—as long as your investment keeps moving higher. If your index fund or stock moves lower and stays lower, the compounding effect won't work as expected until the index or stock recovers.

The longer you hold your investment, the more that compounding works on your behalf. To repeat, compound interest is the interest on both the money you invested and the money earned from that investment. This is how investors like yourself build wealth.

INDEXING: SIMPLE MATH

Another great thing about index funds is the math is so basic. This means you can make money without knowing that much about the financial markets. The indexing strategy is easy to use and understand, and best of all, it works. As long as you don't sell early, you can use index funds to help your child make money in the stock market or pay for their college education.

I'm not telling you this because it sounds good or because I write for a brokerage firm (I don't anymore). I am saying this because I have seen the results. I have seen average folks build fortunes by following the indexing strategy. It happened to several of my friends and neighbors. A relatively small investment in an index fund is a gift that keeps on giving.

WHO ELSE LIKES THE INDEX STRATEGY?

It's not just Bogle who believes in the indexing strategy. In 2013, Warren Buffett wrote a letter to his Berkshire Hathaway shareholders and said that most investors should put their money in a low-cost S&P 500 index fund. Buffett also said that when he passes away, he wants 90% of his money to go into an index fund.

He also said, "I believe that 98% or 99%—maybe more than 99%—of people who invest should extensively diversify and not trade. That leads them to an index fund with very low costs."

And in a 2020 letter to his shareholders, Buffett wrote, "When the dumb investor realizes how dumb he is and invests in an index fund, he becomes smarter than the smartest investor. Most investors, both institutional and individual, will find the best way to own common stocks is through an index fund which charges minimal fees."

In 2023, the late successful investor Charlie Munger (and Buffett's partner) said in an interview with the *Wall Street Journal*, "Most people should not do anything other than have index funds. That is a perfectly rational thing to do for somebody who just does not want to think much about it and has no reason to think he has any advantage as a stock picker. … Why should he try and pick his own stocks? He does not design his own electric motors and his egg beater."

INDEXING RISKS

I have spent a long time explaining all of the great things about index funds. To be fair, I'd also like to tell you about some of the risks.

First, when buying index funds (or stocks for that matter), there is always the chance that the market will decline. That is the risk that all investors take. If the market goes down for a long time period, you may wonder if the index-buying strategy was such a great idea.

Once again, a more painful drop is when the market falls by more than 20%. This is a bear market. In the worst bear markets, the market could fall by far more than 20%. It is not a pleasant experience to look at your account and see big losses. In fact, it is scary for many investors.

When there is a bear market or correction, a lot of people panic or worry they will lose all of their money. Truthfully, there is no need to worry about temporary pullbacks. When the market recovers eventually (the overall stock market has *always* recovered), then the index fund will be worth even more. Why? Because you wisely continued to invest new money as prices fell. I've done the math: you should be very pleased with your investment when the volatility ends and it's smooth sailing ahead.

WHAT SOME CRITICS SAY ABOUT INDEXING

Some traders claim that index funds are boring, and they're correct. Index funds rarely make huge moves during the day (unlike some stocks, which can be much more volatile). Therefore, index funds will not meet the needs of anyone looking for fast money or entertainment.

Think about the children's story, the tortoise and the hare. Although the hare was faster and stronger, the slow-and-steady tortoise won the race. Relating it to the stock market, an index fund is the tortoise. You are likely to win the race and beat the hare, but it takes a long time.

Another criticism of investing in index funds is the same for all investments: although it's great to make money, you may have to pay taxes on the *capital gains* (i.e., realized profits). *Capital gains* is a fancy term that means you made a profit from any investment.

> Note: If you're concerned about the tax consequences of index funds, talk to your broker or a tax accountant.

REMINDER: DON'T SELL

One problem with holding index funds is the temptation to take the money out of the account, especially if the stock market crashes or if there is a major correction. That would be a mistake, but it is a mistake that many people make.

During your child's life, there should be several stock market crashes, approximately one every 10 years (but these crashes could be longer or shorter, and each is different). Corrections of approximately 10% are much more common.

It makes some investors nervous when the market makes violent moves. As an investor, it's best to ignore day-to-day stock market *volatility* and keep holding the index fund. Bottom line: encourage your child not to sell the index fund no matter what the market is doing.

CONSENSUS: INDEXING IS A WINNING STRATEGY

John Bogle was right: the indexing strategy is the best one for most people who don't have time to watch the market every day. If you are a beginner, I urge you to start with a so-called boring, passive index fund.

Indexing is not rocket science. As mentioned previously, I have acquaintances who used this strategy to make good money. My neighbor, Alan, started indexing when he was in his 40s, and now 25 years later, he has nearly a million dollars in his S&P 500 index fund. Imagine if he had started when he was even younger.

Recently, my doctor thanked me for recommending the S&P index fund a few years ago. She told me that her portfolio "quadrupled" during the last 10 years because she listened to me. (To be fair, she also invested in a biotech stock that turned out to be a big winner, which helped supercharge her returns.)

There is nothing wrong with what my doctor did. She bought an index fund as her core holding and then set aside a small sum to buy a higher-risk stock. In my doctor's case, the biotech stock was wildly successful. If it had been a loser, it would not have been a disaster because most of her money was parked in an index fund.

My dentist used a different approach. He put several thousand dollars into an S&P 500 index fund many years ago and never added to it. He said it's worth well over a million dollars now. If my dentist had used the *dollar cost averaging* strategy, his account would be worth much more. The main point is that buying and holding an index fund has made many people very wealthy.

How Long Does It Take to Become a Millionaire?

To find out how long it takes to become a millionaire by investing in an index fund or any investment, type "Bankrate calculators" in a search engine. On the Bankrate (www.bankrate.com) website, scroll to the investment calculator.

Enter your investment goal, the rate of return, and the amount you want to invest. The calculator will tell you how long it will take to become a millionaire. As you'll learn from using the calculator, if you invest in a tax-free or tax-deferred plan, your child will be wealthier several decades earlier than those who invest in a taxable account.

Therefore, take any opportunity to put your child's money (and your own) into a tax-deferred or tax-free plan. (You will learn more about tax-free plans such as the Roth IRA in Chapter 6.)

To be specific, your child could have over a million dollars before age 59½, assuming a conservative 7% annual return. (Many say that a 10% annual return is more realistic when investing in the S&P 500 based on an annual average return since 1928.) The challenge: your child will have to contribute at least $2,500 a year to reach the million dollars.

Let's assume you start by investing a lump sum of $100 for your child but add $200 every month into a taxable account ($2,400 annually). Assuming a 7% annual return on the investment, in 50 years, your child will have almost $1,000,000 in a tax-deferred account. In a taxable account, nearly $500,000 will be waiting for them at retirement thanks to compounding and dividends.

In the first 20 years, the account grows by "only" $98,776 in a tax-deferred account, but the effect of compounding kicks into high gear after that, and the account takes off, making your child a millionaire over the next 30 years. If you change the annual return to a more aggressive 10%, your child will have $1,000,000 after only 40 years.

Even if your child contributes $1,200 per year ($100 per month) and earns 7%, they will have over $500,000 after 50 years in a tax-deferred account. If the investment earns a more traditional 10% per year, in 46 years, they'll have almost $1,000,000.

Idea: Set a goal for yourself and your child to make $1 million. Write that number on an index card and post it on a wall or bulletin board. List the investment products you plan to buy beginning with the S&P 500 index fund. If you believe in the power of positive thinking, compounding, and dollar cost averaging, you can achieve this goal. A tax-deferred account will help you reach this goal even faster.

CONCLUSION

Now that I may have convinced you to invest in an S&P 500 index fund, the next decision is which index product to buy. There are actually two main types of index funds, and I'll describe both in Chapter 4.

CHAPTER FOUR

INDEX ETFs AND MUTUAL FUNDS

By now, I hope you see that buying and holding an *index fund* is an excellent strategy. Not surprisingly, there are several ways to buy them. The two most popular methods are explained in this chapter. This may seem confusing at first, especially if you are new to the financial markets.

After I describe how to buy an index fund, I'll explain which index products I consider to be the best. Obviously, you may choose other indexes to trade, and that's fine. The main goal should be to buy and hold an index, no matter which one you select.

Following are the two main index products that enable you to buy the S&P 500 index. They are an S&P 500 *exchange-traded fund (ETF)* or an S&P 500 *mutual fund*. Both are popular choices.

It can seem a little mind-boggling because there are so many S&P 500 index products. For example, each brokerage firm and almost every mutual fund company has their own version of the S&P 500 ETF or mutual fund.

So, you may ask, what is the difference between an index ETF and index mutual fund?

INTRODUCING THE S&P 500 INDEX ETF

One of the most common ways to invest money into the S&P 500 index fund is to buy it as an *ETF* (*exchange-traded fund*). ETFs have exploded in popularity, and for good reason. ETFs contain a basket of securities that track a specific index or sector.

You can buy an ETF that tracks sectors within the economy (e.g., technology, telecommunications, retail). You can also buy ETFs by asset class (e.g., stocks, bonds, fixed income). Whatever financial product you are interested in, there is probably an ETF that meets your needs. There is even an ETF devoted to trading cryptocurrencies such as Bitcoin.

There are thousands of ETFs, and new ones are created each year. If you don't want to take any risks at all, you can buy *fixed-income* ETFs, which include a number of low-risk financial products, including nearly risk-free *Treasuries*.

If you are interested in buying stocks of overseas companies, there are ETFs that track the stock market of nearly any country in the world. For example, you can buy a German ETF, France ETF, British ETF, South or North American ETF, European ETF, or an Asian, Middle Eastern, or African ETF.

The interesting fact about ETFs is that they trade just like stocks. That means you can buy or sell ETFs whenever the market is open.

Although there are tons of ETFs, the most popular track the major stock indexes (i.e., index ETFs).

The following three index ETFs are well liked because expenses are low, they are diversified, and they track the S&P 500. Even better, the S&P 500 index ETF funds listed here are easy to buy or sell (i.e., they are *liquid*). However, there are other excellent index ETF funds not listed here as well.

- Vanguard S&P 500 ETF (symbol: VOO): A popular ETF with low expenses and no minimum investment.
- BlackRock S&P 500 ETF (symbol: IVV): One of the largest ETFs that tracks the S&P 500. No minimum investment and expenses are low.
- SPDR S&P 500 ETF (symbol: SPY): This ETF tracks the S&P 500 index. SPY is always one of the most actively traded ETFs on the NYSE. It doesn't cost much to buy (expenses are low). It also has the highest daily volume of any ETF. This ETF is very *liquid*, which means you can buy and sell it quickly at competitive prices.

Note: SPY was the original ETF that tracked the S&P 500, a revolutionary idea when it was created in 1993. At first, investors were reluctant to invest in SPY, but three years later, the fund's assets soared above $1 billion dollars. Recently, SPY had more than $400 billion in assets. Don't be surprised when it rises above $500 billion. SPY pays a dividend, which is distributed quarterly.

- Invesco QQQ ETF (symbol: QQQ): Instead of buying SPY, you or your child can buy QQQ. This ETF tracks the Nasdaq-100 index and includes 100 mostly technology stocks.

To review, the main advantages to buying an ETF index fund are that expenses are low, there is no minimum investment, and you can buy or sell the ETF at any time during the day. For all of these reasons, index ETFs are an excellent idea.

> Hint: To see a current list of the most popular S&P 500 index funds, in a search engine, type "rank top S&P 500 ETF index funds" followed by the current year.

S&P 500 INDEX ETFs AREN'T PERFECT

Although ETFs that track the S&P 500 is the most convenient way to buy the S&P 500 index, there are risks. First, if the price of the ETF declines, you'll lose money. Obviously, some years will be profitable, and other years not so much.

After decades of owning an index fund, however, the odds are good that an S&P 500 index ETF will be higher than when you bought it (but no one can guarantee that). The best idea is to teach your child to buy and hold the index ETF.

In fact, because index ETFs trade like stocks, some people may be tempted to trade them rather than being an investor. You may buy an index ETF as a long-term investment, but it could be appealing to constantly buy and sell them rather than holding for the long term. This is not recommended.

It's also possible that a few children, as they get older, may want to be active traders, a time-consuming and difficult strategy. If they insist on trading in addition to investing, suggest that they start with a very small sum and most of all, leave the index fund alone.

INTRODUCING S&P 500 INDEX MUTUAL FUNDS

There is another way to invest in an S&P 500 index fund, and that is through a *mutual fund*. Here's how mutual funds work: an investment company creates a portfolio by pooling investors' money. They use the cash received from investors to buy a variety of stocks, bonds, fixed income products, and indexes such as the S&P 500.

Following are three highly rated S&P 500 index mutual funds that will get you started, but there are many more excellent mutual funds not listed here as well.

Each of these mutual funds has no minimum investment and comes with low fees.

- Vanguard 500 Index Fund Investor Shares (symbol: VFINX)
- Schwab S&P 500 Index Fund (symbol: SWPPX)
- Fidelity 500 Index Fund (symbol: FXAIX)

Hint: If you want a current list of the most popular S&P 500 index mutual funds, in a search engine, type "rank S&P 500 index mutual funds" followed by the current year.

INDEX ETFs VERSUS INDEX MUTUAL FUNDS

Although an index mutual fund is similar to an index ETF, there are some differences. For example, an index ETF can be bought and sold during market hours, whereas an index mutual fund can only be bought and sold at the end of the day.

Just as with an ETF, an index mutual fund pools investors' money. If one or more stocks in the mutual fund does poorly, it will barely affect the overall performance of the entire fund. That's diversification.

Fortunately, most index mutual funds have low expenses, instant diversification, and low *portfolio turnover* (this means that the fund manager changes the portfolio only a few times per year because stocks in the index changed).

Which is better, an index ETF or index mutual fund? Because of low costs and no minimum investment, the ETF may be a smarter choice for many people, but in the end, it's your decision. An index mutual fund with low expenses and no minimums is just as good a product as an ETF index fund.

> Note: Because the index ETF and the index mutual fund are so similar, moving forward I'll refer to these products as *index funds*. Choose which index fund best meets your needs, whether it is an ETF or a mutual fund.

INVESTING IN (NON-INDEX) ETFs

The only ETFs discussed so far are index ETFs. The most popular ETFs track the major stock indexes such as SPY and QQQ. There are also ETFs that track the stocks in the Dow Jones Industrial Average (symbol: DIA), and the Russell 2000 (symbol: IWM).

Once you're comfortable investing in an S&P 500 index fund, following are other ETFs that you may find interesting. These ETFs may have an active manager (they buy and sell the stocks in their ETF) or a passive manager (they only buy stocks in the ETF, but don't trade them).

Dividend (or Income) ETFs

Wise investors know that *dividend-paying* stocks are a good idea. When you own *dividend stocks*, as a shareholder, you receive money in the form of *dividends*. Typically, the cash received from the dividends is reinvested into additional ETF shares. Dividend-paying stocks are often the more stable "blue-chip" companies.

Those who prefer to own less-risky stocks tend to buy ETFs that own dividend-paying stocks. Examples of dividend-paying ETFs include the following (but there are many more not listed here, so do your research):

- SPDR S&P Dividend ETF (symbol: SDY)
- ProShares S&P Technology Dividend Aristocrats ETF (symbol: TDY)
- ProShares Russell US Dividend Growers ETF (symbol: TMDV)
- ProShares S&P 500 Dividend Aristocrats ETF (symbol: NOBL)

> Note: Dividend aristocrats are companies that have increased their dividends by at least 25 consecutive years.

Bond ETFs

Bonds are not easy for most people to understand. Briefly, bonds are a fixed-income product issued by a corporation or government to raise money (i.e., capital). Bondholders invest in bonds to earn higher interest rates than are available from banks. The corporation or government promises to repay the cost of the bond in full with interest.

Buying individual bonds is a rather complex process with a number of risks, usually related to interest rates (or in a worst case, default). For example, when interest rates are rising, bonds lose value. However, when interest rates are falling, bonds are more valuable.

Fortunately, instead of buying individual bonds, you can buy a bond ETF (or a bond mutual fund). This way, you let a skilled ETF manager buy bonds for you. If the manager is a good bond picker, then the value of the ETF rises. Note: Not all bond ETFs have an active manager that picks bonds. Bond ETF index funds typically have passive managers who only follow the bond index.

To get started, here is a list of highly rated bond ETFs you may want to consider, but there are many more not listed here as well:

- Fidelity Total Bond ETF (symbol: FBND)
- iShares Core Total USD Bond Market ETF (symbol: IUSB)
- iShares Core U.S. Aggregate Bond ETF (symbol: AGG)
- Vanguard Tax-Exempt Bond Index Fund ETF (symbol: VTEB)
- Vanguard Total Bond Market ETF (symbol: BND)

Should you or your children buy bonds? Many financial advisors believe that investors should have some bonds in their portfolio in addition to index funds. The percentage to allocate to bonds, if any, is a personal decision. Typically, bond buyers are more concerned about risk than growth. More than likely, however, your children will be buying more growth stocks (and ETFs) and fewer bonds.

> Note: For a current list of top bond ETFs, in a search engine, type "rank top bond ETFs" followed by the current year. The performance of the top bond ETFs constantly changes, so look for ETFs with excellent 3-, 5-, and 10-year records.

Treasuries

Treasuries are considered to be one of the safest investments in the world because they are backed by the "full faith and credit" of the US government. Investors who buy Treasuries don't want to lose money.

In return for safety, interest rates and returns are lower. It's a fair trade: Treasury buyers are willing to accept lower returns with a promise they will not lose money.

Although you can buy US Treasuries directly from the government (at TreasuryDirect.gov), it's even easier to buy a Treasury ETF (or a Treasury mutual fund) from your brokerage firm. With a Treasury ETF, you are buying a basket of high-quality Treasury bonds with a range of *maturity dates* (i.e., the date when the government must repay the money they borrowed).

Another advantage of buying a Treasury ETF is the same as buying any ETF: liquidity, diversification, and lower costs. Also, Treasury ETFs pay out dividends to shareholders each month. (Suggestion: Reinvest those interest payments.)

Here are a handful of Treasury ETFs with low expenses that you may want to study. For a full list, type "rank top Treasury ETFs" followed by the current year. A list of independent sources that list the top Treasury ETFs will be displayed.

- iShares U.S. Treasury Bond ETF (symbol: GOVT)
- U.S. Treasury 10-Year Note ETF (symbol: UTEN)
- Global X 1–3 Month T-Bill ETF (symbol: CLIP)
- iShares 20+ Year Treasury Bond ETF (symbol: TLT)
- Schwab U.S. TIPS ETF (symbol: SCHP)

Note: There are three categories of government bonds: *Treasury bonds*, *Treasury notes*, and *Treasury bills*. Bonds have maturity dates of 10 to 30 years. Notes have maturity dates ranging from 1 to 10 years. Bills have the shortest maturity dates, from 1 to 12 months. Usually, the longer the term of the loan, the higher the *yield* (i.e., the annualized return on your investment).

INVESTING IN (NON-INDEX) MUTUAL FUNDS

You are already familiar with index mutual funds. Now, let's discuss buying non-index mutual funds. Although mutual funds are similar to ETFs, there are a number of differences.

As you recall, when buying mutual funds, buying and selling decisions are up to the mutual fund manager(s). They choose stocks or other products they believe will outperform the indexes.

There are mutual funds for every possible strategy, country, or industry. For example, some mutual funds invest in stocks (i.e., stock fund). Other mutual funds invest in sectors (e.g., technology, retail, or real estate). Many invest in bonds (e.g., bond fund, Treasuries), international stocks (i.e., international fund), and commodities (e.g., gold, silver, soybeans, etc.). Just like ETFs, you can own shares of a mutual fund that holds only dividend-paying stocks.

Mutual funds are an excellent idea for those who want to invest in certain sectors of the market but may not have time to do research. For example, perhaps you or your child want to buy technology stocks but don't have the knowledge to find which stocks are best. By buying shares in a mutual fund, you pay for a professional money manager to choose the best technology stocks. (As you know, you can also buy a low-cost ETF that has the same goal.)

If you are fortunate enough to own shares in a mutual fund managed by someone with the rare stock-picking skills of famed investor Peter Lynch, you will do very well, and probably better than the S&P 500.

The skill of the mutual fund manager(s) determines the fund's performance. Therefore, before picking a mutual fund, look at the fund manager's record for the last 3, 5, or 10 years. Hopefully, the manager beat the S&P 500 more times than not.

Your brokerage firm has a full list of all of the mutual funds. There are thousands of them, each with its own goal and strategy. Once you find the right mutual fund, you may decide to hold it as long as you like (forever, for some investors).

Mutual funds are popular investments. For a minimum investment (ranging from a few hundred dollars to $3,000 or more), you can invest in a basket of stocks that meet your needs.

If you buy a mutual fund, choose a *no-load* (i.e., no sales commission) fund with low fees. However, avoid *load funds*, which charge higher sales charges. Load funds with high management fees have a hard time outperforming the S&P 500 and other indexes, one of the reasons that no-load funds are a better idea.

Here are a few of the top-rated *mutual fund families* you may want to consider (in any order), but there are hundreds more: Vanguard, Fidelity, PIMCO, American, Franklin Templeton, Invesco, T. Rowe Price, and BlackRock, to name a few.

Note: For a current list of the top mutual funds, type in a search engine "rank top mutual funds" followed by the current year. As you know, there is no guarantee that these mutual funds will continue to outperform. That's why I suggest you choose mutual funds with excellent 3-, 5-, and 10-year performance results.

Morningstar (www.morningstar.com) is an excellent resource for mutual fund investors. They provide detailed information about every mutual fund, including the total assets in the fund. Obviously, funds with more assets are the most popular (but not always the best performing). Morningstar also includes a one- to five-star rating for each fund.

THE MATH BEHIND MUTUAL FUNDS

Unlike a stock or ETF, mutual funds use a different method for calculating the share price. The daily fund value is based on the closing price of each of the fund's investments. Stocks and ETFs also publish the final closing price, but it is the last trade of the day on the stock exchange.

Your brokerage account lists the *net asset value* or *NAV* for each mutual fund each day. Once the NAV is known, the fund calculates the number of shares you get for your money (i.e., the fund multiplies the current NAV by the number of shares owned.). For example, if you have $100 to invest, and the NAV is $14.54, you get 6.878 shares.

Another example: Let's say you want to buy $300 worth of ZYX mutual fund. Log into the brokerage account and type in the mutual fund's symbol. Enter the amount you want to invest (in this case, $300), and press the Buy button.

Your broker transfers $300 from your cash account to that of the mutual fund. The purchase is made after the market closes for the day and after the NAV is determined.

You can buy any mutual fund through your broker or send cash directly to the fund company. Every mutual fund company has a website and instructions on how to open and fund an account. Nevertheless, it's easiest to buy mutual funds (or any financial product) through your broker.

PROBLEMS WITH MUTUAL FUNDS

Like any investment, mutual funds are not perfect. As I've written before (more than once!), at least 80% to 90% of mutual fund managers fail to beat the S&P 500 each year. If you buy a *load fund* with extra fees, it's even harder for the fund manager to outperform the market.

Another drawback to mutual funds is a rule that forces you to hold the fund position for at least 30 days before you are allowed to sell. If you sell within 30 days, you may be penalized with a *redemption fee*. With stocks and ETFs, you can buy and sell anytime within the market day without penalties. Obviously, a mutual fund is aimed at long-term investors who have no intention of selling their fund quickly.

Another negative about mutual funds is the same as with index funds: diversification limits how much you can earn. For example, let's say you own shares of a mutual fund that owns Google stock. If Google's share price zoomed 10% higher one day, instead of earning the 10% return you dreamed about, your daily profit will be far less. And if the entire market went down that day even as Google soared, your mutual fund investment could lose money.

Why? Because no matter how well the mutual fund did on any given day, its price can never increase (in percentage terms) by more than the best stock in the portfolio.

Another negative is that some mutual funds, especially the most specialized, exotic ones, charge high fees, high minimums, and have high expenses. Because the fund manager wants to be paid for their stock-picking skills, expect to pay extra fees, from .05% of the cash invested to as high as 10%.

CONCLUSION

In the end, it's your decision whether mutual funds or ETFs meet your needs, and those of your child. Again, the simplest strategy is to own an S&P 500 index fund, either as an ETF or mutual fund.

In Chapter 5, I introduce several indexing strategies that worked in the past, and the one rule that will help you and your child keep your money for a lifetime.

CHAPTER FIVE
STRATEGIES, RULES, AND RISKS

This is one of the most important chapters in the book. It is where I show you how to make money with indexing using index ETFs or mutual funds.

DOLLAR COST AVERAGING

To make the indexing strategy work, invest a certain amount of money into the S&P 500 index fund each month. Decide on a sum that you can afford to set aside that is not needed for expenses. It can be as little or as much as you are comfortable with. The important part is not how much you put into the account. Instead, it's to get your child in the habit of saving money every month. As your child grows older, they can increase the amount they invest.

There is a name for this popular strategy: *dollar cost averaging (DCA)*. It involves investing the same amount of money over equal time periods, typically a month (but you can choose your own time frame).

Here's the great thing about the DCA strategy: when the index price falls, you buy more shares with the same amount of money. When the index price rises, you are buying fewer shares that month.

For example, let's say you invest $50 into an S&P 500 index fund when it's at $400 per share. The next month, if the price drops to $379 per share, invest another $50. Keep investing the same amount of money each month no matter whether the market is up or down. Over the long term, the math is favorable when using this strategy. The small number of extra shares you acquire really adds up.

Let's say in a worst-case scenario, the market plunges by 30% during a one-month period. With dollar cost averaging, instead of panicking, you simply invest the same $50 that month but with a 30% discount. As the market climbs higher over time, the extra shares you purchased will make a big difference in the value of your account.

If you teach your child the dollar cost averaging strategy, they won't fear down markets. Obviously, markets don't always go higher, and when it falls, dollar cost averaging shines.

As your children get older, teach them to think of the money invested as another bill they need to pay. But in this case, they are paying themselves rather than someone else.

This method of dollar cost averaging into the stock market is better than simply dumping a lump sum of money into the market at one time. In my book, *Understanding Stocks*, I did the math. Dollar cost averaging beats out the *lump-sum method* almost every time. (The only exception is if you were lucky enough to invest at a market bottom.)

The money your children put into the market every month is a ticket to a better, richer life. The alternative is putting money into a savings account. Unfortunately, no one ever got rich storing cash in a savings account. As mentioned, after 30 years, the money invested in the bank is still sitting there earning compound interest, but missing out on dividends or a rising stock market. Because of inflation, the money in a savings account will be worth a lot less in buying power.

> Important note: Dollar cost averaging works as long as you keep investing a set amount of money no matter whether the market is up or down. That means when the market is falling hard and everyone around you is panicking, keep investing money into the index fund.

GIFTS AND ALLOWANCES

When your child receives a gift from a relative, or gets an allowance, or makes money at a job, teach them to put some of that money into an index fund. It's a small sacrifice but worth it. When your child is older, they will be thankful that they embraced this healthy financial habit.

Should they use their money to buy the latest electronic game, computer, or smartphone, or should they invest? The answer is to do both. By all means, buy the things they want or need, but also set aside some money for investments.

When your children start to see their investment account grow each year, they will see the light. Perhaps their investment will lose value some years. That's life in the financial world. But when the investment bounces back and moves even higher, they will learn that investing really does build wealth, although slowly at first.

AUTOMATE THE MONTHLY DEPOSITS

Some parents *automate* the investment by instructing their bank or employer to transfer a certain amount automatically. For example, you can set it up so the bank or employer automatically transfers $25 or $50 from your account into an index fund each month. Increase the transferred amount as your income grows.

If your child is interested, show them how the value of their index fund rises and falls with the stock market. Some children may be so fascinated by the market (and watching their money increase over time) that they may want to learn more. Perhaps they will take finance or business classes in college. This is possible because you introduced them to investments at an early age.

Note: To automatically transfer money from your bank account or employer to your brokerage account for the first time, look for a tab such as "Move Money" or "Transfer Money." After selecting this tab, select "Online Transfer" or "Transfer." Select "Setup Transfer." This enables you to transfer cash from your external account such as a bank account to the brokerage account.

However, when setting it up for the first time, there is one more step that many people don't realize. Next, you must set up an automatic transfer from the cash account in your brokerage account to the index fund such as the S&P 500 (or a stock).

Choose the time period you want, such as monthly. If done correctly, each month the amount chosen will be transferred from your bank to a cash account at the brokerage firm. Then that amount will be transferred from the cash account to an investment such as an index fund.

Call the brokerage firm if you have any questions about automating your monthly investments.

HOW IS YOUR INDEX FUND DOING?

After buying shares of an index fund, there is no reason to pay too much attention to it, unless you want to. To find the current value of the account, and how much money you made or lost (i.e., profit and loss), log into your brokerage account and look at the front screen. The total investment, gains and losses, will be listed at the top of the page along with how the stock market is doing that day.

At first, some children may want to check their account every day. Eventually, they may want to check it every few months or every year. Another educational opportunity appears when there is a major market event such as a correction or crash, or even a huge rally. Then your child may be curious as to how their index fund did on that day, and that's good.

INTRODUCING ONE RULE

Throughout the book, I continued to say that to be a successful indexer, you and your child should follow some rules. The most important rule is **don't sell.** If you obey this rule, it is very likely your child will have a sizeable nest egg waiting for them when they are older. Not selling an index fund is the most important rule when investing for the long term. Put money into an index fund, but the money should not be taken out. Even after your child turns 18 years old, that money should be **untouchable.** That also means not panicking or switching strategies no matter what happens to the stock market. Stick to the dollar cost averaging strategy that made your child money in the first place.

If that money is taken out of the account, it's never coming back (even if it was spent wisely). In addition, some of the advantages of owning an index fund disappear when withdrawals are made, including earning compound interest, dividends, and future investment income.

If you can follow this one basic rule and not sell your shares, your child will receive all of the benefits that an index fund provides.

I have personally learned the hard way that once money is withdrawn from an index fund, it's not returning anytime soon, if ever. Sometimes when the account gets large (over $100,000, for example), some older kids find an excuse to withdraw money. In fact, the biggest mistake your child can make is to take money out of the account, or worse, liquidate the entire fund.

For the index strategy to work, the money should not be touched with only a few exceptions (see next section). Follow the no-withdrawal rule and later in life your child will be pleasantly surprised at the sizeable sum of money that is waiting for them.

Bottom line: don't sell—an index fund is a keeper.

EXCEPTION: SHOULD YOU *EVER* SELL AN INDEX FUND?

Although you should not sell the index fund, there are a few exceptions. First, if you invest in an educational plan for your child (such as the 529 plan explained in Chapter 6), it's designed so that money can be taken out of the fund and used for educational purposes such as tuition and books.

Another reason to sell is if you need the money to buy a house. In that case, by all means withdraw some money, but continue to invest new cash into the index fund every month.

Finally, if there is a terrible emergency, and you must withdraw some money, then it must be done. Keep in mind the consequences that the money will probably not return. In addition, there may be tax consequences when selling.

Hint: Investing in an index fund using the dollar cost averaging strategy is a commonsense method used to generate wealth. It is not designed to create instant riches like in the lottery or a casino. Explain to your child that buying an index fund is a way of investing in their future. It will take a while to make money, so be patient.

CREATE AN EMERGENCY FUND

Adults should have a cash emergency fund that is separate from their investments, ideally a money market fund at a brokerage firm or bank. This money must be instantly available and used when the car breaks down, if there is a medical problem, or an unexpected expense comes out of left field. One of your goals, even before investing in stocks, is to have a comfortable cash cushion.

You may want to teach your children to have an emergency fund (a cash stash stored in a safe place to be used in case of emergency). Yes, the world has mostly gone digital, but it's amazing how often cash is needed when least expected.

INTERVIEW WITH JOHN BOGLE, CREATOR OF THE FIRST INDEX FUND

By now, I hope you're convinced that the most effective strategy for your child is investing in the S&P 500 index fund.

Before we move to the next chapter, I want to share with you an interview I did with the late John Bogle, founder and former CEO of the Vanguard Group. As you remember, he created the world's first index fund, and was one of its biggest supporters. By the time you finish reading the interview, I'm sure you'll be even more certain of the value of investing in index funds.

In the interview, Mr. Bogle shared excellent insights about the index fund strategy. And now, here is the Mr. Bogle interview of a few years ago. (Portions of this interview were also included in my book, *Understanding Stocks* (McGraw-Hill).)

Sincere: When did you first come up with the idea of index fund investing?

Bogle: It goes back to 1951, when I was at Princeton University. I wrote my senior thesis on the mutual fund industry. I examined many funds and studied their data. From my research, which I admit was somewhat superficial, I concluded that it was difficult, if not impossible, for mutual funds to consistently outperform the market averages. For me, that's where it began.

Sincere: How did you start the first index fund at Vanguard?

Bogle: By the time Vanguard started in 1974, we were in an ideal position to bring out the world's first index fund. I was inspired by a 1974 article in the *Journal of Portfolio Management* by economist Paul Samuelson, who was one of the greatest economists of the 20th century. He challenged anyone to find "brute evidence" that active managers can beat the market. He pleaded for the creation of an index fund. In 1975, my first major business decision at Vanguard was starting the world's first index mutual fund, and Dr. Samuelson was my greatest supporter. He followed up by writing a four-page article in *Newsweek* in which he said that his prayers were answered. It was important for me to have his support.

Sincere: Did the mutual fund industry follow your lead?

Bogle: Not at first. There was a poster circulating around Wall Street that said, "Index Funds Are Un-American!" The mutual fund industry didn't understand why anyone would want to be average. Also, most people in the industry were not looking to lower costs for investors; rather, their goal was to increase revenues for mutual fund management companies by gathering assets and raising fees. It wasn't until the 1990s that index funds started to grow.

Sincere: Why do you like indexing?

Bogle: Index funds take the cost out of the system and guarantee investors their fair share of stock market returns. It's simple, although for some people it might be boring.

Sincere: How should someone start with an index fund?

Bogle: If you get out of college and are able to put a couple of hundred dollars away in an index fund, which is the only intelligent choice, you'll learn how markets work. You'll learn what happens when prices go down and learn about the wisdom of a buy-and-hold strategy. Don't try to time the market. Simply stick to a disciplined, long-term investment strategy. Invest whatever you can afford to save every month, and don't worry about what the market is doing. It doesn't matter.

Sincere: What do you think about index ETF funds?

Bogle: I don't know if I approve or disapprove. If you were to buy an ETF such as SPY (SPDR S&P 500) or VTI (Vanguard Total Stock Market ETF), there is no reason why you can't buy and hold. The cost of holding an ETF and what I call a traditional index fund is about the same. The difference is that with an ETF, you can trade all day long, which you cannot do with a traditional index fund. So we must ask ourselves this question: Is that an opportunity or a curse? I would say it's a curse. The idea of trading "all day long, in real time," is just silly.

Sincere: You believe strongly in buy and hold. What if you see a bear market coming? Should you still hold?

Bogle: Yes. First, you should be properly diversified, and your asset allocation must be right. Sixty percent stocks and 40% bonds is a good place to start. If you see a bear market developing in advance, you must get out at the height of the market and jump back when it hits its lows. But I don't know anyone who can tell you precisely when a bear market is going to begin, and I certainly can't tell you when it's going to end. That means you have to be right twice. The chances of that are so small that you should just stick to your long-term investment plan. It's great advice to tell me to get out of stocks before a bear market. But can you drop me a note when it's time to get back in? I think investors should stay the course whether it's a bear market or not. Don't try to outsmart the market.

Sincere: What if there is a huge drop in the stock market?

Bogle: When the market suffers a 50% drop, people panic and think about getting out. Their emotions lead them in the wrong direction. Don't fall for that trap. Simply continue to invest every month without worrying about the momentary movement of stock prices. Just look at the quarterly statements, and over the course of an investment life span, you'll be overwhelmingly satisfied with your returns. You'll see that you fared much better than most other people who let their emotions get the better of them.

Sincere: What do you suggest?

Bogle: Don't pay too much attention to the daily gyrations of the stock market. If you have a diversified portfolio with low costs, simply stay the course. Yes, you would have been right if you got out at the high and back in at the low, but not only do I not know anybody who actually did so; I don't know anyone who knows anyone who did it.

Sincere: Should you ever sell?

Bogle: Gradually, as you get into your 30s and 40s and you have more money at stake, you should begin to diversify some of your assets in equity index funds and invest in a bond index fund. You want to change your allocation gradually by reducing your stock portfolios and building your bond position. Historically, bond index funds have generally had higher yields than stock index funds, although that will not always be the case.

Sincere: Should investors buy and hold individual stocks?

Bogle: If you are one of those rare, fortunate people who know how to pick winners, by all means you should definitely buy good stocks and forget indexing. But I don't know how to do that. The record is quite clear that, in many cases, what we thought were good stocks can turn out to be disasters. Look at it this way: people like to gamble, and investors are no exceptions. The math is the same on Wall Street as it is in Las Vegas. You bet on red, someone else bets on black, but in the long run, only the house wins. And Wall Street, the croupier in the middle, doesn't care what you do as long as you do something.

Sincere: What about investors who think they can beat the market?

Bogle: First, you should create a long-term investment portfolio with an appropriate mix of stock and bond index funds. This is your serious money account. It's the money you need for retirement. That should be 90% to 95% of your investable assets. It is very boring to watch but exciting when you are ready to retire. Take the other 5% of your assets and use it as "funny money." I recommend creating a separate account for your funny money, and you can trade in that account to your heart's content. Many people have a gambling instinct, and in this account, you can trade individual stocks. After five years, check out the returns and see if you actually beat the market. Did you? I think the chances are not quite zero, but maybe 1% or 2%, that you did.

Sincere: Why doesn't everyone use indexing?

Bogle: The idea of indexing is somewhat counterintuitive. It's the idea that no one is consistently better than the index. If you get a salesperson who says you shouldn't believe the index fund bunk, that his or her fund does better, it can be hard to resist. But the person doesn't tell you that many active fund companies switch managers often. When you include all the additional expenses incurred by actively managed funds, what are the chances that all these asset managers can beat the market? I would say it's not zero, but maybe 0.0001%. But asset managers are great marketers, and they focus only on those funds that beat the market.

Sincere: What is the biggest mistake that investors make?

Bogle: I don't know the biggest, but the lack of diversification is a big mistake, and the lack of asset allocation. Also, don't try to outsmart the market. No one knows more than the market.

Sincere: Any final advice?

Bogle: In the long run, investment return is driven by economics, not emotion. Corporate value increases over time through dividend payments and earnings growth. In the very long run, stock market returns equal corporate returns. In the short term, all bets are off.

Asset Allocation

In the interview, John Bogle spoke about the usefulness of *asset allocation*. Although deciding how much money to divide (or allocate) to each investment may not be exciting to most people, it's important to understand how it works.

An example of asset allocation is investing 65% in stocks, 25% in bonds, 5% in fixed income (i.e., Treasuries), and 5% in a savings account (i.e., cash).

Figuring out the proper allocation is how financial advisors earn their fees. To create this so-called perfect allocation, the advisor may suggest certain financial products based on a number of factors such as risk tolerance, your time frame, and your goals.

There is one problem with creating the so-called perfect portfolio. You need a lot of money to buy all of these products! That is why for many people, starting with an index fund is the simplest and most efficient way of participating in the stock market. Is it perfect? No, but it's still one of the best strategies ever created for many, if not most, people.

In fact, if you own a diversified index fund, and have cash on the side for emergencies, it's hard to go wrong. Should you own bonds? Many financial experts believe you should, so you may decide to invest in a bond mutual fund or bond ETF. Guess what? Your asset allocation problem may have been solved.

Nevertheless, when the market is falling by 10% in one day, and all of your money is invested in one stock, or even an index fund, you will feel the pain of losing money. Asset allocation helps to reduce this pain.

CONCLUSION

If you have read this far, you already know a lot about index funds. In Chapter 6, I'll tell you about a number of plans for children or relatives under 18 years old, especially educational plans to help pay for tuition and college expenses in the United States. They are designed to not only to save money but also help defer or shelter taxes. (Fortunately, most of these plans allow you to invest in index funds, including the S&P 500.)

If you are interested in these educational plans, keep reading, because I'll do my best to make them understandable. However, if you're *not* interested in these plans, feel free to skip Chapter 6. Perhaps you already created a savings plan for your child or want to open a brokerage account in your name only.

CHAPTER SIX

529 PLAN, ROTH IRA, AND UGMA

Before I wrote this chapter, I spent a long time talking to brokerage firms and different state governments to make sure I gave you the most accurate information. One thing that I learned: these overlapping educational plans can be confusing! My goal was to cut through the confusion and provide insights into which account meets the needs of your children.

Admittedly, this chapter can be a bit overwhelming to some readers so you may want to read it slowly. Also, if you are not interested in any of these accounts, or live outside the United States, feel free to skip this chapter and move to Part II, where I discuss buying and selling individual stocks.

Note: Before enrolling your child in any of these plans, call the brokerage firm, financial advisor, or state government. The representatives will give you the most up-to-date information and tell you if any of the rules and regulations have changed.

OVERVIEW OF COLLEGE SAVINGS PLANS

There are several college savings plans that are designed to help your child pay for college. The most popular is the *529 plan*, which is offered by brokerage firms as well as state governments, but with some differences. The name *529* comes from Section 529 of the federal tax code.

The main 529 plan is the *529 educational savings plan*, also known as a *college savings plan*. It's a little confusing because nearly every brokerage firm and almost every state has a different name for these plans. Fortunately, almost all include *529* in their titles. It enables parents to save money for college, and do it tax-free. The best part is that it is *not* limited to your own state, and it can be used for any eligible college.

Specifically, the 529 educational savings plan enables parents to set aside money to help pay for tuition or any educational expenses from kindergarten through graduate school. Educational expenses include tuition, room and board, and supplies. A huge advantage of this plan is the tax benefits. The money in this plan grows tax-free as long as it is used for educational expenses.

Another advantage: the plan owner (which is probably you) controls the investments in the account and all future educational expenses.

Guess what? The 529 plan is funded by investing after-tax money into certain products such as index funds and mutual funds. Your child's education is paid for with the tax-free gains made from these products. However, there are a limited number of investments that are allowed. For example, with a 529 plan, the owner (e.g., the parent) is not allowed to buy individual stocks.

The educational savings plan is ideal for parents or other relatives who want to help pay for a child's education. Following are some of the main points of the 529 educational savings plan.

- The child is allowed to use tax-free investments from the 529 plan to pay for tuition and other qualified educational expenses such as textbooks and living expenses.
- Anyone can open a 529 plan by filling out an application, but they are usually created by parents or other relatives on behalf of the child. The child is the beneficiary (the person who gets all of the benefits from the 529 plan). Once the account is open, relatives or friends can be asked to give cash gifts to the plan on birthdays or at other important events. You can also make lump-sum contributions or monthly deposits.
- The 529 plan can be purchased from a brokerage firm, financial institution, or from the state. Every state except one offers the 529 college savings plan. Most brokerage firms and states have a dedicated team of 529 specialists who will answer all your questions. Note: The names of state 529 plans are noted at the end of this list.
- The 529 college savings is controlled by the parent indefinitely. The owner has the flexibility to decide how the money is spent and whether money should be withdrawn (there are penalties and tax consequences if the money is taken out early or if not used for educational purposes).
- Another advantage of the 529 plan is if your child decides not to go to college, you can change beneficiaries, pass the plan to other children, or find other ways to use the money other than for college

(i.e., vocational school, graduate degree, etc.). The money can remain in the plan indefinitely.

- The money in the 529 plan is allowed to grow tax-free until it is withdrawn. Even better, as long as the money in the account is used for educational expenses, there shouldn't be any state or federal taxes (but talk to your broker or a tax advisor to confirm). Nevertheless, tax-free withdrawals from the plan are limited to a certain amount.

- Similar to any long-term investment, the earlier the child is enrolled in this plan, the better. This gives the investment more time to grow. Find out your investment choices. It is very likely that the S&P 500 index fund will be one of the choices, but you should check to make sure.

- Find out the fees for creating the 529 plan. The cost should be extremely low, especially if it is opened directly with your brokerage firm or state government. If bought through a financial advisor, however, it could be more expensive, primarily if they charge "maintenance fees" or even worse, a percentage of the investment. Suggestion: Avoid buying plans with these extra charges.

- One of the biggest drawbacks to the 529 plan is the money in the account must be used *only* for educational purposes, that is, to pay for tuition, books, and supplies. If not used for educational purposes, there may be penalties and taxes.

- The 529 plan regulations often change so understand the most current rules with your broker or financial advisor. Each brokerage, and state government, has variations of these products, including hybrid plans. You want to choose a plan that meets the needs of your child.

- Another reason for opening a 529 plan is for "accelerated gift giving," another way of saying that you can contribute much more money to the 529 plan (compared to other tax-free plans) while avoiding a red flag from the IRS. Nevertheless, there are yearly caps on how much can be invested into the account without tax consequences.

- To apply for any of these plans, go on your brokerage firm or state government's website. All of the information needed to open the 529 will be there, including the latest rules on contribution limits and Roth IRA rollovers.

Because each state has its own rules, fees, and benefits, be sure to go on your home state's website to find out what the state plans offer. Most states have colorful websites with tons of details about the plans and the advantages of enrolling with them as well as minimum and maximum contributions to the plan.

In alphabetical order, here are the names of the states that offer the 529 educational savings plan (college savings plan). Before enrolling in any plan, compare the state plans with the plans offered by brokerage firms.

Alabama (CollegeCounts 529), Alaska (Alaska 529), Arizona (AZ 529), Arkansas (Arkansas Brighter Future 529), California (ScholarShare 529), Colorado (CollegeInvest 529), Connecticut (Connecticut Higher Education Trust (CHET) 529), Delaware (DE529), District of Columbia (DC College Savings Plan), Florida (Florida 529 Savings Plan), Georgia (Path2College 529 Plan), Hawaii (HI529), Idaho (Ideal Savings Plan), Illinois (Bright Start 529 Plan), Indiana (CollegeChoice 529), Iowa (College Savings Iowa), Kansas (Learning Quest 529 Savings Plan), Kentucky (KY Saves 529), Louisiana (START Saving), Maine (NextGen 529), Maryland (Maryland 529), Massachusetts (U.Fund 529), Michigan (Michigan Education Savings Program (MESP)), Minnesota (MNSaves), Mississippi (Mississippi Affordable College Savings (MACS)), Missouri (MOST 529), Montana (Achieve Montana), Nebraska (Nebraska Educational Savings Plan Trust (NEST) 529)),

Nevada (Nevada's College Savings Plan), New Hampshire (UNIQUE College Investing Plan), New Jersey (NJBest), New Mexico (The Education Plan), New York (New York's 529), North Carolina (NC 529), North Dakota (College SAVE), Ohio (Ohio's College Advantage 529), Oklahoma (Oklahoma 529 College Savings Plan), Oregon (Oregon College Savings Plan), Pennsylvania (PA 529), Rhode Island (CollegeBound Saver), South Carolina (Future Scholar), South Dakota (CollegeAccess 529), Tennessee (TNStars), Texas (Texas College Savings), Utah (my529), Vermont (Vermont Higher Education Investment Plan (VHEIP)), Virginia (Virginia529), Washington (DreamAhead), West Virginia (SMART529), and Wisconsin (Edvest).

PREPAID TUITION PLANS

Prepaid tuition plans lock in future tuition payments for in-state schools by purchasing tuition credits. Your child (the beneficiary) can use those credits later when they attend a participating, in-state school. Because prepaid tuition plans have more rules and restrictions, they are less popular than the 529 savings plan.

Only nine states offer the *prepaid tuition plan*, including Florida, Maryland, Massachusetts, Michigan, Mississippi, Nevada, Pennsylvania, Texas, and Washington. To find more information about these plans, type in your state name followed by "prepaid tuition plan."

Here are a few highlights of the prepaid tuition plan:

- The prepaid tuition plan guarantees your child's tuition at the current rate for a public university or college. In other words, this plan guarantees that your child will pay today's tuition when they go to college in the future. There should also be tax breaks with the prepaid tuition plan, including credits and tax deductions. The prepaid tuition plan is not an investment plan. It simply guarantees tuition for in-state colleges.

- This plan restricts which colleges children may attend. However, if a child wants to attend an out-of-state school, they can, but they must pay the difference between the in-state credit hours and the out-of-state credit hours.

- In some states, it's possible the account holder will lose their prepaid tuition if they move out of state. Be sure to discuss all of the rules with a state prepaid tuition plan specialist before enrolling in the plan.

- Parents can have both a 529 plan and the prepaid tuition plan (if your state offers it).

- Prepaid tuition plans can be used only for tuition and *not* for other expenses such as room and board, books, or other educational expenses.

- Before enrolling in the prepaid tuition plan, check with your state to find out the most recent changes, if any, and if there are any restrictions not mentioned here.

THE ROTH IRA

One of the most brilliant tax-free plans in the United States is the Roth IRA. (The other brilliant plan is the 401(k), where employees contribute part of their salary for a tax-deferred retirement.)

You can open a Roth IRA for yourself in a brokerage account, or for your child in a *custodial Roth IRA* (see next). After your child turns 18 years old, they can open a tax-free Roth IRA on their own.

The Roth IRA is funded by contributing after-tax dollars up to a certain limit. The investments, along with all gains, are tax-free, and can be withdrawn without penalties as long as you follow some simple rules.

The only downside to the Roth IRA is there are income restrictions. You also don't receive immediate tax benefits because you're using after-tax dollars.

Generally speaking, most financial advisors believe that the Roth IRA is a better choice for most people than a traditional IRA because of how withdrawals are taxed. With a traditional IRA, you'll need to pay income taxes on any withdrawals that are made. With the Roth IRA, once retirement age is reached, both the earnings and contributions can be withdrawn tax-free.

Note: To find more information about the Roth IRA, or any other tax-free or tax-deferred plan, visit irs.gov (search for Roth IRA), or visit any online brokerage firm website. They will have plenty of information about these plans.

CUSTODIAL ROTH IRA (FOR CHILDREN)

Another popular plan for children under 18 years old is a *custodial Roth IRA*, where all assets are controlled by the custodian (you or another relative) until the child turns 18 (or 21 in some states). Although brokerages may have different names for the Roth IRA (such as Roth IRA for Kids), if your child is under 18 years old, it must be a *custodial* account.

Opening a Roth IRA is a great way to teach children about the importance of saving and investing money received from work, and watching that money grow tax-free over their lifetime.

The only catch to the custodial Roth IRA is in order to qualify, the child must have "earned income." Financial experts mention how the children of movie stars and singers receive income by working for their famous parents.

Fortunately, you don't have to be a movie star to help your child build tax-free wealth with a custodial Roth IRA. Babysitting jobs, mowing lawns, and dog walking enables your child to qualify for the custodial Roth IRA. If your child works for you, that income also qualifies.

There are limits to how much can be contributed each year. The most recent limit is $7,000 beginning in 2024, but that is sure to increase in the future. If your 9-year-old child invests $6,500 per year into a custodial Roth IRA, they would end up with a $2.8 million tax-free windfall by the time they are 59½ (assuming a conservative 7% annual return). This amount varies depending on how old your child is now, how many years they will be adding to the account, and the growth rate.

As your child's account grows in value, they may experience the thrill of making money when the market moves higher, or the disappointment of losing money when the market falls. The odds are good, however, that the account will grow substantially along with your child.

If they continue to invest income into the tax-free Roth IRA, and not withdraw the money, your child is very likely to be a millionaire before retirement (if they choose to retire). Perhaps this will motivate them to start investing now.

DOWNSIDE TO A CUSTODIAL ROTH IRA

Unfortunately, it may be hard to convince many children not to withdraw cash that they want for games, apps, or phones. Older teens may want to withdraw money in the Roth IRA to pay for a car or for a vacation.

Therefore, the biggest negative to a custodial Roth IRA may occur when your child takes control of the account at 18 or 21 years old (depending on the state they live in). As soon as they are adults, they have the right to use the money as they wish. By the way, when they are no longer minors, the custodial Roth IRA turns into a standard tax-free Roth IRA. The account remains with them.

If your child leaves that money undisturbed until they are 59½ or older, it won't be a problem. If they take the earnings out early, in addition to missing out on the future investment returns, there will be early withdrawal penalties (typically 10% of the amount withdrawn). They can always withdraw the original investment at any age without being hit with a 10% withdrawal penalty.

Once again, it is critical to teach your child from an early age that the money invested in these accounts is intended for the long term and that it is a bad idea (financially) to touch that money, even after they turn 18 or 21 years old.

UGMA (UNIFORM GIFTS TO MINORS ACTS)

This strange name, *UGMA*, is actually a *custodial brokerage account* for minors under the age of 18 or 25 (depending on the state in which they live). Because it's an individual brokerage account, any gains on the investment are taxable. With this plan, the minor (anyone under 18 years old) can receive cash, stocks, bonds, mutual funds, and other liquid financial assets.

In other words, an UGMA is designed to transfer wealth to a minor.

At first glance, UGMA seems like an excellent idea. As with any custodial account, UGMA is controlled by an adult custodian until the child turns 18 or 25, when the custodian transfers the account to them. The 18- or 25-year-old is now in full control.

The attractive part of this plan it is a less time-consuming way of transferring assets to your children without having to create a *trust*. UGMA is easy to set up and is flexible, especially in the hands of a competent attorney.

When opening a custodial account for your child, it becomes attached to their Social Security number. That means that any profits or taxes from the account will be in your child's name. It is a gift, one that can't be rescinded (taken back). Once your child turns 18 or 25, they become the legal owner of the custodial account and can do what they want with the money.

WHY CREATE AN UGMA

One of the advantages of an UGMA is that there are many more investment choices than for a 529, for example. With a 529 plan, the money must be used for educational purposes, which may include only five or six investment choices (most likely an index fund and various mutual funds).

UGMA may also be a good idea if you want other family members to make a gift to your child, using after-tax money, into a brokerage account (although there are limits to how much can be contributed). All you have to do is provide the relative (such as grandparents) the account number, and the grandparent can deposit money into the account. Be sure to remind your relatives that it is an "irrevocable" gift that can't be taken back.

Obviously, you can contribute to the account as well. You can always look for reasons to add money to the fund (such as a birthday gift).

Once again, when your child turns 18 or 25, they will have access to the cash. If they were taught not to touch that money for any reason, then they may have a large nest egg waiting for them as they get older. If they withdraw that money for questionable purchases, you may wonder if opening an UGMA was a good idea.

Here's a real-life example: Your child's grandparents set up an UGMA for your child so they can contribute money into the account on birthdays and other special occasions. Their goal is to teach your child the value of investing as well as helping build an investment account. Perhaps when your child is older, the grandparents may want to convert the UGMA to an UGMA 529 plan, but that day is far away.

Although the custodial account sounds like a wonderful idea, it is far from perfect.

DISADVANTAGES OF UGMA

Although an UGMA is relatively easy to set up, there are a number of tax rules that were created that make the UGMA less appealing. For example, there are now strict limits on how much gift money can be sheltered from taxes (an amount that will change as the years go by).

Also, when setting up an UGMA, taxes on the earnings are paid for by either the child or parent at the child's lower tax rate. Because of tax consequences, it's important to talk to a tax professional or broker to get the facts.

One of the reasons there are strict tax rules regarding UGMA is that in the past, some parents used these accounts to shield their own income. These parents transferred money into their child's account not out of the kindness of their heart but to hide income from the IRS. As a result, the IRS created a number of strict rules on how the UGMA is managed.

> Note: Another method for keeping control of family money, especially as the investment grows, is to set up a *trust*. Trusts are more complex than an UGMA, so consult a tax accountant or lawyer if taking this route.

Also, if an index fund makes too much money (that's good, right?), there could be tax consequences for your child.

UGMA NEGATIVELY IMPACTS FINANCIAL AID

Another downside to UGMA is how a college considers the custodial account when the child is applying for financial aid. When your child is ready for college, the investment account, which is probably worth a lot more than the original deposit, will count as an asset owned by your child. This may reduce the financial aid your child receives. Suddenly, that UGMA is a liability in this circumstance (In fact, UGMA counts approximately seven times more heavily against the family in the aid formula than a 529 account. For that reason alone, the 529 may be a better choice for most people).

WHAT HAPPENS AFTER YOUR CHILD TURNS 18 YEARS OLD?

As mentioned several times, the biggest problem with the UGMA is that once your child turns 18 or 25, all of the money in the account is legally theirs. If your child is disciplined and patient, then the custodial account can be a huge bonus.

However, if your child takes every cent of the UGMA as soon as they turn 18 and blows it on fun stuff, they will miss out on the really big profits that would have come if they hadn't spent it.

Bottom line: for most parents, it probably makes more sense to open a 529 educational plan than an UGMA because you are in control of the account, and it limits how the money can be spent. A Roth IRA is also an excellent idea.

UGMA Versus UTMA

There is another custodial account, *Uniform Transfers to Minors Act (UTMA)*, that some parents may want to consider. Although an UGMA account limits the transfer of assets to financial products such as cash, stocks, bonds, and mutual funds, an UTMA allows the beneficiary to receive property, for example, real estate and fine art.

Before opening any custodial account, talk to your broker or other professional. If the plans seem too complicated, and they can be, there are other choices. As mentioned, you can open a brokerage account for yourself. After your child turns 18, with your financial help, they can open their own account.

THE UGMA 529 PLAN

A less popular version of the 529 plan is the UGMA 529 plan, another *custodial plan*, in which an adult is in charge of the fund for any child under 18 years old (the beneficiary). Just as with the 529 plan, the money in the account must be used for approved educational expenses. Once the child turns 18 or 25, the child assumes control of the account. If they don't use the money for approved educational expenses, there will be penalties.

The purpose of the UGMA 529 is to enable you (or a grandparent or other relative) to open an investment account for your child as a way to help pay for their education. The question you may ask is, Why open an UGMA 529 instead of a standard 529 where the child controls the account at 18 or 25 years old?

Answer: In some cases, perhaps a grandparent or parent doesn't want to take control of the plan so they just leave it to the child to manage. It happens. In general, however, the standard 529 plan appears to make the most sense because you control the funds.

> Note: A little known fact is you can convert a regular UGMA to an UGMA 529. In this case, the money in the UGMA will be earmarked only for educational purposes. Some parents may want to do this if they are worried their child may withdraw all of the money in the UGMA.

CONCLUSION

Whew! This concludes our discussion about the 529 plan, the Roth IRA, and UGMA. For some of you, this may be as far as you want to go in the book. You can open a 529 educational plan for your child and a brokerage account for yourself (and your child), and invest in an S&P 500 index fund.

The index fund will be your core investment account. Invest in it for a lifetime, and you and your child should build wealth over the long term (especially if invested in a tax-free account). One of the easiest paths to making profits is investing in index funds.

In Part II, however, I discuss different types of investments, including buying and selling individual stocks, and especially how to find winning stocks that will help generate income for years, if not decades. I am sure that many of you want to boost your portfolio by investing in individual stocks, and I will show you how.

However, if you have no desire to participate in the stock market, feel free to stop reading and buy shares of an index fund. You can always return to Part II if and when you're ready. This is a personal choice. Putting it into school terms, Part I is "required reading," while Part II is "extra credit."

For those who want to learn how to buy and sell stocks, you have come to the right place. Investing in stocks is a completely different experience from buying index funds. I did my best to make it a fascinating journey.

PART II

BUILD WEALTH WITH STOCKS

Many of you have patiently waited for this section. This is where you will learn how to build wealth by buying individual stocks. As you already learned, investing in an index fund makes sense. Index funds are easy to understand and may give slow and steady returns over a long time period. That should be your main account.

However, as you gain more experience, you or your child may want even bigger returns. If you want to boost your yearly performance, you will learn how to do it here.

Remember when I wrote that when buying stocks, you are sharing in the success or failure of a corporation? In other words, when buying shares of stock in Costco or Walmart or Target, if these stores do well, the stock price goes up and you make money. I should emphasize that if you pick certain stocks, you can make a lot more money than by owning an index fund.

However, if a company does poorly and earnings are weak, the stock price goes down and you lose money. In Part II, I tell you how to find and analyze winning stocks, the potential risks and rewards, and the psychological pitfalls that trip up most beginners.

CHAPTER SEVEN

FIND WINNING STOCKS

Many investors want to make money, and that's why they want to invest in stocks. For example, anyone who bought and held shares of Apple (AAPL), Microsoft (MSFT), Alphabet (GOOG), Amazon (AMZN), Nvidia (NVDA), Meta (META), or Tesla (TSLA) did extremely well over a 10-year period. Many became millionaires during this amazing era, when interest rates were low and stocks were at all-time highs.

During the next 10 years, many of these same stocks will probably continue to do well, but several may falter as new technology emerges and old technology falls out of favor. We know from history that the good times can't last forever, as many people learn the hard way. Still, there will always be spectacular stocks. Your goal is to try to find them before they surge, which is what I'll help you do in this chapter.

WHAT IF YOU HAD INVESTED $1,000 IN ONE OF THESE STOCKS?

Following are examples that should help you see why buying and holding the stocks of great companies for decades makes sense:

- If you had invested $1,000 in Apple in 2004 and did nothing else, your $1,000 investment would be worth almost $454,000 in 2024, or an annualized total return of 35.8% (https://bit.ly/3Xpp6Nk).
- If you had invested $1,000 in Walmart in 1970 when its shares were made available to the public (through its initial public offering), and did nothing else, your investment would be worth $20,785,447 in 2024 (https://bit.ly/4aYdofH).
- If you had invested $1,000 in Nvidia on Jan. 22, 1999, when Nvidia first went public, and did nothing else, your investment would have increased by approximately 277,708% and be worth close to $2,784,065 in 2024 (https://bit.ly/3XtTar7).
- Finally, if you had invested $1,000 in Nvidia stock in 2004, and did nothing else, your investment would be worth more than $426,000 in 2024, or an annualized total return of 35.4%. The S&P 500, however, produced an annualized total return of "only" 9.9% over the same time period (https://bit.ly/4c0aPuC).

Imagine if you had used the dollar cost averaging strategy and invested a small amount each month in just one of these winning stocks. Guess what? You'd be rich. This is why it's a good idea to find stocks in excellent companies and hold for a lifetime.

However, trading stocks takes more time and skill than simply buying and holding an index fund. Although you can buy and hold stocks, they must be monitored more closely. After all, sometimes even the best stocks can fall out of favor and sink.

Think of once-great companies such as Sears, Blockbuster, JCPenney, Circuit City, Radio Shack, Kodak, General Motors, Borders, Nokia, Chrysler, Enron, Toys"R"Us, WorldCom, Polaroid, Lehman Brothers, Xerox, all of whom went bankrupt. Anyone who bought and held shares of these stocks probably lost a ton of money.

There were a number of reasons why these companies lost money. Perhaps it was poor management, a failure to adjust to new technology, or they didn't excite their customers with the latest products.

Sears, once one of the greatest companies in the world, made all of these mistakes. Sears was the first mail-order company and should have been the first to put their products online. But they didn't. Upper management failed to recognize that the old ways of doing business were over.

Upper management at Sears didn't understand the power of the internet until it was too late. Instead, they stuck to their old brick-and-mortar way of thinking, and eventually their customers went elsewhere. Who needed Sears, for example, when you could buy everything cheaper at Amazon, and have it delivered to your home?

The point is that after you buy shares in a company, you can't go to sleep. With stocks, you must follow the company and its stock more closely. Start by choosing a website that you like, for example, MarketWatch, CNBC, Bloomberg, Yahoo Finance, *Forbes*, *Wall Street Journal*, CNNMoney, and *Financial Times*, to name a few. There are hundreds of great websites to learn about the stocks you buy.

If you don't do your due diligence, it's easy to lose money, especially if the company doesn't keep up with the latest technology or is hit with bad news, such as a poor earnings report. This will cause the stock price to fall.

If you followed my advice, you will open a brokerage account. Perhaps you and your child are already investing a set amount of money into the S&P 500 index fund each month. When you're ready to buy stocks, the market will be waiting for you.

With that in mind, let's step it up a notch and discuss buying individual stocks. Buying stocks is more challenging but also more rewarding because of the potential gains you can make.

WHAT STOCKS SHOULD YOU BUY?

The first step is finding a stock worth buying. That's why we are going to focus on finding winning stocks that can be held not only for years but also for decades. If you choose the right stocks, you and your child will build wealth for yourselves. Choose incorrectly, however, and you will lose money.

The following ideas should help in your journey. Although many investors try to find a needle in a haystack, often the very best companies are in plain sight—if you take the time to look for them.

FIND GREAT STOCKS WHILE SHOPPING

One of the smartest ways to find great stocks to buy is to *think*. Think of the things you buy, the stores you visit, and the stocks in companies that are often in the news.

One of the great stock pickers of the 1990s, Peter Lynch, got his stock ideas by going to the mall and watching where people shopped. That led Lynch to do more research on these companies.

He didn't just buy stocks in companies that were popular. He made sure he was getting a bargain. As I wrote in the introduction, the stock market is like a street market or an auction. Buy great stocks at a reasonably low price and sell at a much higher price in the future.

Let's discuss Sears again. Years ago, if you were at the mall, you may have noticed that while the Apple store was crowded with excited customers, fewer and fewer people shopped at Sears. They had great tools, but so did Home Depot and Lowe's. I'm no fashion expert but their clothes seemed outdated, and prices were not competitive. They'd occasionally have appliance sales to lure customers in, but few stuck around once the sale ended.

These were important clues: while Apple turned into one of the world's greatest technology companies, Sears went bankrupt. You didn't need to look at a balance sheet to see that Sears was in trouble. All you had to do was go shopping.

Therefore, when looking for stocks to buy, be an observer. Look at the stores that are crowded and attract the most attention from customers. That's how some people discovered Disney, Walmart, Home Depot, Costco, Lowe's, Starbucks, Walgreen's, McDonald's, Amazon, CVS, and thousands of other great corporations.

However, why buy stock in companies that have outdated inventory, unhappy or indifferent employees, and empty stores? To be fair, many people buy stocks in failing companies with the hope they will recover. All I'm suggesting is that before buying any stock, pay attention to what is happening at the store, especially if it is brick and mortar.

In the technology arena, you may have noticed Google, Microsoft, Nvidia, Meta, Adobe, and Cisco. Customers wanted their products, and wise (or lucky) investors bought their stocks. Guess what? These investors made a fortune, especially if they bought and held for the long term.

Even now, there are many more stocks like these. You just have to go out and find them. Many are in plain sight, if you take the time to look, and study. I'm not saying this is easy, but here are a few ideas to get you started.

BUY STOCKS THAT PAY DIVIDENDS

Although I mentioned dividend-paying ETFs in Chapter 4, let's continue the discussion. Dividend (or income) stocks return money to their shareholders in the form of *dividends*. Corporations that pay dividends are typically large, well-established companies.

Many investors purposely seek out stocks that pay dividends. Typically, those nearing retirement prefer dividend stocks because they provide an income stream (i.e., money flow). Many older folks live off of those dividends. Also, people who don't like taking big risks prefer dividend stocks because they want to buy stocks in higher-quality companies.

Dividend stocks are not just for older folks. They may also be ideal investments for you and your child. Buying dividend stocks is a fantastic idea, and reinvesting those dividends is an excellent way of bringing in consistent income.

You can choose to have the dividend payments deposited into your brokerage account so you can automatically buy more shares, or you can take the dividends in cash. Obviously, the more shares you own, the higher your dividend payment.

Keep in mind that corporations are not required to pay dividends to shareholders, but they will do so if it fits in with the goals of the corporation. Companies that pay dividends often increase the dividend over time, which is a very positive event for shareholders.

ARISTOCRATS AND KINGS

Companies that increased their stock dividend for at least 25 consecutive years are called *dividend aristocrats*. When a company has increased its stock dividend every year over a 50-year period, it is called a *dividend king*.

These solid, dependable companies may not be in the most exciting industries, and rarely get a lot of attention, but for 25 to 50 years they have paid out ever-increasing dividends, enriching their investors.

Dividend aristocrats include Exxon Mobil, Walgreens, IBM, and Caterpillar, to name a few. Dividend kings include Walmart, Procter & Gamble, 3M, Coca-Cola, Johnson & Johnson, Colgate-Palmolive, Hormel Foods, Sysco, Illinois Tool Works, Abbott Labs, Tootsie Roll, Lowe's, and Middlesex Water. To find an updated list of the dividend kings or dividend aristocrats, do an online search.

Note: As mentioned previously, instead of buying dividend stocks, you can also purchase ETFs or buy mutual fund shares that own shares of the dividend aristocrats. A notable ETF is the S&P 500 Dividend Aristocrats (symbol: SPDAUDP). Another ETF with only dividend-paying stocks is the S&P 500 Dividend Aristocrats ETF (symbol: NOBL).

RISKS OF INVESTING IN DIVIDEND STOCKS

Although buying dividend-paying stocks is a good idea for investors interested in income and relative safety, there are a few negatives. First, just because you own a dividend stock doesn't mean the price won't fall.

At times, dividend-paying stocks sink, costing their shareholders. One example is General Electric (GE), once one of the longest dividend-paying stocks in history. After GE's stock price plunged in 2018, the CEO was forced to slash dividends from 12 cents per share to only 1 cent. Adding insult to injury, GE was kicked out of the Dow Jones Industrial Average (DJIA) index because they were a poor representative of the index (but mostly likely because of their performance).

Investors who depended on GE for dividend income lost money on the stock as well as their dividend income. It was a shock to the investment world because GE had been making hefty dividend payments to their shareholders for more than 100 years.

Note: The good news is that GE's stock price and dividend has recovered quite nicely in recent years. This is typical of many stocks that go through rough periods—only to recover many years later.

By the way, when a company announces a dividend cut, you may want to consider selling the stock. It probably means that the company can no longer afford to pay dividends, which may not be a stock you want to own. That is a huge red flag.

Bottom line: When looking for stocks to buy, consider dividend stocks. You receive quarterly dividend payments as long as you hold the stock.

BUY GROWTH STOCKS

A lot of investors are attracted to *growth stocks*, or companies whose earnings increase year after year. Growth companies are expected to grow faster than other companies with better earnings. Investors who like growth stocks want to see fantastic earnings year after year. Not surprisingly, many growth stocks are technology companies.

However, if you buy a growth stock, be prepared for a rollercoaster ride because growth stocks are often *volatile* during the day. It often takes nerves of steel to hold these stocks in your account when the stock price makes large price swings.

The best time to own growth stocks is during a *bull market*, that is, when the overall stock market is moving much higher. Conversely, the worst time to own a growth stock is during a *bear market*, when the stock market is moving much lower. Many growth stocks get a lot of media attention and are often in the news. That sometimes leads to panic buying or selling.

Although it's true that you can make a lot of money owning winning growth stocks, thousands of lesser-known growth companies didn't do so well. Many of these companies lost money for themselves and their shareholders. That is why it's important to learn as much as you can about a growth stock (or any stock) before buying it.

> Note 1: One way of finding a current list of the top growth stocks for the current year is to enter "rank top growth stocks" in your search engine. You will get a list of the best-performing growth stocks for this year (with no guarantee they will continue to outperform).
>
> Note 2: Instead of buying individual growth stocks, you can own shares of a growth ETF or mutual fund. Search for the top growth ETFs by doing a search of "rank top growth ETFs" followed by the current year. Be sure to look at their 3-, 5-, and 10-year performance.

BUY VALUE STOCKS

If the idea of buying growth stocks makes you uncomfortable, you may want to invest in *value stocks*. These stocks are usually less volatile than growth stocks because company earnings are relatively stable (especially when compared to growth stocks). Value stocks got their name because they are stocks that are a "good value" (i.e., they trade at a lower price when compared to their earnings).

Value stocks are often in unexciting companies such as retail stores, banks, and insurance companies. If you invest in a high-quality value stock, plan to hold for a long time (think of years or decades). Although you can build wealth with value stocks, it usually won't happen quickly.

One of the most successful value investors, Warren Buffett, said that he doesn't just buy shares of stock—he is also buying a business. He patiently waits until the stock price is right, that is, when it becomes a good value. He holds them for a long time, supposedly saying that his favorite holding time was "forever" (although he has been known to sell stocks that were not performing well).

This is important: Just because a stock has a low price doesn't mean it's a bargain. Some growth stocks that sell for a very high price are a bargain because they are expected to keep growing. And some value stocks that are cheap may be cheap for a reason, which means you could lose money if you buy the stock.

Note 1: You can look for value stocks by doing an online search. Type "rank top value stocks" in a search engine followed by the current year. You will get a list of the best-performing value stocks for the year. Once again, there are no guarantees that this year's best-performing value stocks will continue to outperform.

Note 2: If you don't have the time to find good value stocks, or believe you lack the skills, consider buying an ETF or mutual fund that specializes in value stocks. Do a search of the "top value ETFs" followed by the current year. A list of the top-performing value ETFs will appear. Check their past performance before buying.

BUY-AND-HOLD: RECOMMENDED FOR BEGINNERS

For most investors, especially beginners, an easy strategy, and one of the most popular, is buy-and-hold. When you combine this strategy with dollar cost averaging, it can provide stock market gains for many years.

The idea behind buy-and-hold is to purchase a stock at a fair price and hold as long as possible. The wonderful part of buy-and-hold is you can watch the value of your stock portfolio rise without constantly analyzing the market (unless you want to).

Investors who bought shares of stock in lesser-known companies such as Cooper Companies (CCO), Pool Corporation (POOL), NVR (NVR), Monster Beverage (MNST), and Deckers Outdoor (DECK) in the early days and held for the long term were richly rewarded for their patience. It wasn't just these stocks that delighted their shareholders—thousands of other stocks too numerous to mention also rewarded their shareholders.

In reality, a lot of these stocks were found through word-of-mouth, financial news articles, and "Buy these stocks now!" columns. Perhaps some of these stocks were found by investors who did some basic research and analysis. Many other investment ideas came from people thinking of the companies they love and the products they buy.

For example, people buy Apple computers or phones; use Microsoft products; fix their houses with stuff bought at Home Depot or Lowe's; watch movies on Netflix; shop online at Amazon; buy groceries at Walmart, Target, and Costco; and use artificial intelligence from Nvidia and Microsoft. Buying shares of stocks in any of these companies made investors a lot of money over the years.

Note: Don't worry if you're still not sure yet how to find great stocks. In Chapter 8, I show you how the experts find winners.

AMAZON: A BUY-AND-HOLD SUCCESS STORY

Here's a true story I included in my book, *Understanding Stocks*. It is a perfect example of how buying and holding one stock for decades can really pay off for long-term investors.

In 1997, a young couple, Mary and Larry, bought *two* shares of a new company, Amazon, an online bookseller. They liked how simple it was to order new books for their young son. They decided to invest in Amazon for their son, but all they could afford was two shares.

For years, their son wanted to sell the shares as the price of Amazon moved higher. His wise parents insisted he continue to hold, and he did. Twenty-four years later, Amazon turned into one of the largest corporations in the world, and the couple's two-share purchase turned into an $81,098 windfall, or a 172,449% increase.

Their son, Ryan, finally convinced his parents to sell some of the 24 shares (the shares had *split* three times, increasing the number of shares they owned) in 2021 to help him buy a house.

Larry and Mary wrote to Jeff Bezos, Amazon CEO, to thank him for creating such a great company. In their letter, they said, "We wished we had bought 10 shares!"

This story shows that you can build wealth with small stock purchases, as long as you choose the right company. Buying and holding great stocks is a strategy that has worked since the stock market was first created.

RISKS OF BUY-AND-HOLD

I wish I could say that buy-and-hold is the perfect strategy guaranteed to make you a millionaire. Unfortunately, there are times when the entire stock market, including your own stocks, plunges. For example, during the 2020 COVID-19 pandemic, stocks in airlines, cruise lines, and travel got hammered as most people stayed home to avoid getting sick.

Before the pandemic, these same stocks had been doing well. And just like that, the pandemic wiped out company earnings and the stocks got punished. If you were a buy-and-hold investor, it would have been frightening to watch shares of your stock fall by 30% or 40%, and sometimes more.

If you followed the buy-and-hold methodology, you would not have sold. But many people panicked and pressed the Sell button. As it turned out, investors who held onto their stock shares were rewarded when the travel stocks rebounded a year later. However, some businesses and their stocks didn't recover, and that's when buy-and-hold fails.

Therefore, one of the risks of buy-and-hold is that people abandon the strategy and sell their holdings—just when they should be buying more shares.

For example, let's say you had bought and held shares of Apple Computer in the 1970s when the company was just getting started. You would have done extremely well until 1985, when Steve Jobs was fired from the company he created. At that time, Apple stock fell to pennies per share as thousands of stockholders dumped Apple shares. The company seemed destined for bankruptcy.

In a surprising development, Steve Jobs returned to Apple in 1997 to rescue the company. Jobs helped make Apple cool again, and the stock didn't stumble until 2000, when its price dropped by over 50% in one day, the biggest one-day decline in its history. (I wonder how many buy-and-hold investors dumped Apple that day.) Apple came roaring back in 2001 when Jobs introduced a revolutionary new product, the iPod, a portable media player. The rest, as they say, is history.

Nevertheless, if shareholders had gritted their teeth and held onto Apple stock through all the ups and downs over the years, they'd be extremely rich. I know someone who did. In fact, every time that Apple plunged, he bought more shares. His buy-and-hold strategy made him a millionaire because he chose the right stock.

The main point is that being a buy-and-holder is not as easy as it sounds. You have to find a winning stock and not let go as you ignore the short-term volatility and noise that makes you second-guess your decision to hold.

Another risk is choosing the wrong stock. After years of holding, you may find that you have lost money. That is always a risk when buying and holding stocks (a major reason why buying index funds makes sense for most investors).

Finally, it takes skill to find stocks that are selling for a fair price and have the potential to move much higher over decades. Buy-and-hold is a wonderful strategy when your stock, and the stock market, are moving higher. When the winds change, and the economy sinks along with stocks, you may wonder whether buy-and-hold was such a good idea.

BUY-AND-HOLD UNTIL SOMETHING CHANGES

One way of reducing risk is to buy-and-hold until something in the company changes. Perhaps there is weak earnings, an unskilled manager, or a stale product. Whatever the reason, if you see problems in the company, it makes sense to sell all or some of your shares. You can always reinvest your money elsewhere, perhaps in a company that is doing better.

This isn't easy to do. Many investors grow so attached to their stocks they don't want to sell. However, buy-and-hold does not mean to buy-and-forget. If you use the buy-and-hold strategy, you must monitor the stock at least every few months. Even though it may be hard to sell a stock that has made you money, it's often wise to cut your losses and sell.

Bottom line: During a long bull market, buying and holding forever seems to be a brilliant strategy. During bear markets, or if you choose the wrong stock, the buy-and-hold strategy will not feel so great. That is why it is so important to choose the right stocks and monitor positions.

HIGH-RISK, HIGH-REWARD STRATEGIES: NOT RECOMMENDED FOR MOST INVESTORS

Sure, there are strategies that can give huge short-term returns, but there is a problem. These trading strategies are so risky it's easy to lose some or all of your investment. Risky strategies include short-term trading such as *day trading* or buying *penny stocks* (i.e., stocks worth less than $3 per share).

Day trading, or intra-day trading, means selling the shares within minutes or hours after buying, and never holding overnight. The goal is to make quick profits. Day trading gets a lot of media attention, but in real life, it's a very difficult strategy. It's the complete opposite of investing for the long term.

There are other short-term strategies such as *swing trading* (holding for a week), *position trading* (holding for one to three months), or trading in *cryptocurrencies* such as Bitcoin (see Chapter 12). These are also high-risk strategies but not as risky as day trading or trading the pennies.

As your child gets older, it's possible they may want to experiment with one of these higher-risk strategies. These ideas should be discouraged because they are the opposite of the long-term buy-and-hold strategy recommended in this book. Unfortunately, it's easy to cross over to the gambling side of investing and blow up an account when using any of the high-risk strategies.

CONCLUSION

Now that you have a better idea of how to find winning stocks, in Chapter 8, I'm going to reveal how three experts find great stocks, each with their own method. It goes to show there is more than one way to make money in the stock market.

CHAPTER EIGHT

HOW THE EXPERTS FIND WINNERS

I n this chapter, I'll introduce three expert investors, all three who are extremely wealthy, all because of the investment strategies they used. Not surprisingly, they made their fortunes mainly by buying and selling individual stocks.

The investment insights from these experts are fascinating because each has a method that works for them.

HOW PETER LYNCH FINDS WINNING STOCKS

I've been fortunate to have interviewed well-known investor Peter Lynch multiple times, considered by many as the greatest mutual fund manager in history. Lynch ran the multibillion-dollar Fidelity Magellan Fund, which averaged an amazing 29.2% average yearly return for over 13 years (beating 99% of all equity funds at that time). That is the reason that Lynch reached legendary status among investors in the 1990s.

Lynch is well known for creating the saying, "Invest in what you know," which suggests that investors buy stocks in companies that they know well. For Lynch, this means going to the mall or to an individual store and seeing which ones had the biggest crowds. That's how he got some of his investment ideas.

Just as Warren Buffett stated in Chapter 7, Lynch also says he isn't just buying a stock but is buying a company. Therefore, if a company's profits increase, the stock price should increase. Lynch says that over the longer term, there is a 100% correlation between a company's profits and its stock price.

He explains: "If corporate profits go up for the next 10 years, the stock market will be higher. And if corporate profits decline for the next 10 years, the stock market will be lower. It is profits that drive the stock market."

Here are a few of the strategies that Lynch uses.

Lynch Strategy 1: Find Companies with Good Stories

The key to Lynch's success was finding companies that were profitable and were superior to the competition. "I worked very hard every day to find a really good story. If you look at enough stocks and view enough companies, eventually you will find something. The person who overturns the most rocks wins the game."

Lynch Strategy 2: Visit the Company

Lynch is well known not only for going to the mall searching for ideas but also for visiting a company's place of business. For example, before buying stock in an automobile company, he went to automobile dealerships and spoke with the salespeople, checked the cars, and walked around the lots. For Lynch, knowing how a company operates in real life is as important as its stock price.

Lynch Strategy 3: Do Research on the Stocks You Want to Purchase

A lot of people misunderstood what Lynch meant by "invest in what you know." He stresses that it doesn't mean going to the mall or to a store and then going home and buying shares in a company that is popular. "That's not doing research," he says. "Investing in what you know is valid, but you must still do your own research. If you aren't willing to do the research, then don't buy the stock. You'd be better off buying a mutual fund."

He quips that many people do more research when buying an airplane ticket than they do when buying a stock.

Lynch Strategy 4: Think of the Reasons Why You Want to Own the Stock

Before buying a stock, Lynch suggests you think of four or five reasons why you want that stock. "You don't invest $10,000 in some stock because you heard about it on the bus or at a party, but know nothing about it. It's possible the company is doing well, but perhaps it has a lot of debt."

Lynch says there are tons of opportunities to find great stocks, if you're willing to take the time to look. He mentions how well Home Depot did, and then how Lowe's also succeeded. "Lowe's was also able to prosper," he says. "They had excellent stores and also captured a large market share of that industry."

Lynch Strategy 5: Study the Bond Market for Clues

Lynch suggests looking at bond prices to see what the bond market thinks the company is worth. "If bonds are selling for as little as 30 or 40 cents on the dollar, that tells you the bond market thinks the company would go bankrupt." In this example, he would not buy the stock. "On the other hand," he says, "if a stock appears to be doing poorly but the bond market thinks the company is doing fine, that is a good signal."

Lynch Strategy 6: Don't Panic If the Stock Market Goes Down

Lynch says not to panic during bear markets, when the stock market (and some of your stocks) may go down by 20% or 25%. "If you understand the companies you own and who their competitors are, you're in good shape. You don't panic if the market declines and your stock goes down. If you don't understand what a company does and the stock price falls by half, what should you do? If you haven't done your research, you might as well call a psychic hotline for investment advice."

Lynch adds that if you are an investor who panics because your stock fell by 10% or 20%, you shouldn't be in the stock market in the first place. "More money has been lost worrying about corrections than by the correction itself," he notes.

The key, he says, is to ignore the negative background noise. "If the market goes down by 10% or more, the talk shows are negative, the news shows are negative, and there is a lot of pessimism. By 7:15 a.m. you're already in a bad mood."

What should you do if the market dives? He told me: "As long as you don't need the money in the next 10, 20, or 30 years for a wedding or your kid's college, I would be comfortable about being in the stock market. This is what makes a good investor." He says that sometimes the best time to buy or add to your stock position is when the market and the economy seem terrible. He admits that it takes a strong stomach to buy when it appears that everyone else is selling.

In summary, Lynch says that you should do basic research on companies before buying shares in their stock. Also, understand why you want to buy the stock in the first place, and keep an eye on the stock's financials to make sure it is still making money.

HOW WARREN KAPLAN FINDS WINNING STOCKS

While many investors have heard of Warren Buffett, few have heard of another successful investor, Warren Kaplan. Kaplan is a buy-and-hold investor with more than 73 years of stock-investing experience. You can learn a lot from someone who started with nothing, and then made a fortune in the stock market.

Growing up in a poor family in the Bronx, New York, Kaplan uses six uncomplicated stock market strategies that have helped him and his family build a very comfortable life in Florida. Several of the strategies he uses have been mentioned in this book.

Kaplan Strategy 1: Buy Dividend Aristocrat Stocks

Kaplan loves to buy the dividend aristocrats, or stocks that have raised dividends for 25 years or more consecutive years. "By paying a meaningful dividend of at least 3% or 4%," Kaplan says, "it shows that the board of directors understands its responsibility to shareholders when compared to companies that don't pay dividends and instead pay huge salaries to executives."

There are a number of things that Kaplan studies before buying a stock. First, he looks at the *price/earnings ratio (P/E ratio)*, which helps him determine whether a stock is selling for a reasonable price. This tool is used by value investors such as Kaplan to find high-quality companies that are on sale.

However, P/E ratios are not the only tool for selecting investments. For example, a stock with a low P/E may not be a bargain, whereas a stock with a high P/E may actually be very fairly priced. That is why the P/E ratio should be considered as only one data point before investing in a stock. But also look at other data in addition to the P/E.

Kaplan also looks closely at the company's dividend history. "I want a company that is truly committed to raising their dividends," he says. "I don't care about the last three years, but if the company raises its dividends for a number of years, that means something to me. That is a stock I'll put on my watch list. You have to be patient and wait to buy at a price that represents good value."

Before buying a stock, Kaplan suggests that investors buy a small number of shares of the aristocrat stocks. "Instead of buying 100 shares of a $40 stock, buy 10 shares for $400. This is what I still do now." He adds: "Getting the right buy price is more important than anything else," which he admits can be challenging.

Kaplan Strategy 2: Buy Dividend-Paying ETFs

Kaplan is a strong believer in ETFs, so he focuses on those that contain dividend stocks. Several of the ETFs that he liked were mentioned previously, including ProShares S&P 500 Dividend Aristocrats ETF (NOBL),

SPDR S&P Dividend ETF (SDY), ProShares S&P Technology Dividend Aristocrats ETF (TDV), and ProShares Russell US Dividend Growers ETF (TMDV).

Kaplan also likes ETFs that include technology companies that have increased their dividends for at least the past seven years. Such stocks include IBM (IBM), Cisco Systems (CSCO), Apple (AAPL), and Microsoft (MSFT). He buys the stock directly or buys an ETF that contains these stocks.

Kaplan Strategy 3: Buy-and-Hold Until Something Negative Happens

Unlike many investors who buy and hold forever, Kaplan holds stocks until something negative occurs in the company. It could be a change in management, earnings, or a dividend cut. If any of these events occur, Kaplan may reduce his holdings or sell all of his shares.

Although it's fine to be a long-term investor, Kaplan says, it doesn't mean holding indefinitely. That is why he's always looking at the stocks he owns and evaluates whether they are still worth holding.

When does Kaplan sell his stocks? "I may sell if the tone of the market is not right, or if the dividend yield is moving too low. My intention is to buy those same stocks back at lower prices."

He admits that he doesn't like to sell too often, but will sell if he must. He often uses the options market to complete the sale. "I sell like I buy," he says. "A little at a time."

Kaplan Strategy 4: Sell Covered Call Options

Kaplan sells *covered call options* on the dividend-paying stocks that he owns. This conservative money-making strategy enables investors to receive extra income just by holding the stocks that they own. In a way, they are acting like a landlord who receives rent payments.

When selling covered calls, if the stock he owns is automatically sold (according to the option rules, it is *called away*), Kaplan usually reinvests into another stock using the profits he just received.

Kaplan explains why he likes this strategy: "Selling covered calls is an effective method to receive extra income while earning additional profits as the stock rises. It never bothers me when a stock I own moves higher and is called away. I can always buy the shares again."

Note: If you want to learn more about options, I wrote a book for beginners, *Understanding Options*, that describes the most profitable option strategies, including selling covered calls.

Kaplan Strategy 5: Buy Stocks at Lower Prices

Unlike many investors, Kaplan is not bothered when the market moves lower. This gives him a chance to buy his favorite stocks at reduced prices. "I may start by buying six shares of an aristocrat stock, and if it goes lower, I buy another eight or nine more shares depending on the stock price."

Kaplan also has ideas of what to do during a *bear market* (when the entire stock market has fallen by at least 20%). "I have a larger than normal cash position during a bear market," he says. "The lower the stock price, the greater the bargain I am getting. You have to be patient when investing during a bear market. However, even during the worst bear market, the stock market is not going to zero. That's why you must learn to control your fears."

Nevertheless, Kaplan is very aware of the damage that bear markets cause. "I am sometimes asked, 'What is the worst bear market?' I always answer: "The one I am in!"

Kaplan Strategy 6:
Keep a Lot of Cash

There is an old Wall Street saying that "cash is trash." However, Kaplan likes to hold cash. "You might be getting only 1% when inflation is at 7%," he says, "but my 1% return is a much better deal than losing far more than 1% when a stock falls by 20% to 50%. Some people complain about losing 7% to inflation when their stock is losing 40%."

Bottom line: Because Kaplan has more than 70 years of investing success, it is wise to consider some of his strategies when buying stocks. He told me that "the key to great investing is to set a goal regarding how much money you need to earn. Once you reach your goal, look to protect your position and income. What I learned after a lifetime of investments is that every loss is a learning lesson. Regardless of your circumstances, you can be financially independent."

HOW WARREN BUFFETT FINDS WINNING STOCKS

Many people consider billionaire Warren Buffett to be one of the greatest investors of all time. He is the CEO of Berkshire Hathaway, a company that owns large share positions in a lot of other companies such as insurance, publishing, and manufacturing. Buffett has also been known to buy stocks in companies such as Apple Computer, Coca-Cola, Kraft-Heinz, and American Express. Buffett and his team of analysts are skilled at finding great companies at reasonable prices.

Known as a buy-and-hold investor, Buffett says that he likes to buy stocks in companies and hold "forever" (although he admittedly sells his stocks when they are not performing well). Buffett prefers to buy stocks that are easy to understand. He once said that if he can't figure out how a company makes its money, he won't buy its stock.

Obviously, Buffett isn't perfect. In the 1990s, he avoided buying most internet stocks because he thought they were too expensive. However, in 2000 when many internet stocks went bust, Buffett had the last laugh.

In a 1977 shareholder letter to Berkshire shareholders, Buffett summarized how he picks stocks: "We want the business to be (1) one that we can understand, (2) with favorable long-term prospects, (3) operated by honest and competent people, and (4) available at a very attractive price. We ordinarily make no attempt to buy equities for anticipated favorable stock price behavior in the short term. In fact, if their business experience continues to satisfy us, we welcome lower market prices of stocks we own as an opportunity to acquire even more of a good thing at a better price."

If you want to copy Warren Buffett, it's easy to do. Several books have been written about his down-to-earth, honest investment ideas. Also, his current stock portfolio is posted on the internet, which can be found if you do a search.

If you find a stock that Buffett owns, don't make the mistake of immediately buying it. First, do your own research. Study the balance sheet and other important financial information. Then go to one of the research websites listed in this book to get a quick overview of the company.

CONCLUSION

Hopefully, you got a few stock ideas from the experts we discussed in this chapter. You may have noticed that each investor has their own strategy for buying stocks. As you gain experience, you can create your own strategies, or copy one of the experts.

In Chapter 9, I discuss two ways of evaluating whether a specific stock is a good investment idea. By using *fundamental* and *technical analysis*, you can evaluate whether the stock is worth buying. Fortunately, I tell you what you need to know without overwhelming you (at least I hope so). Admittedly, this is not an easy chapter.

CHAPTER NINE

ANALYZING STOCKS

U ntil now, I did my best to make investing an uncomplicated experience. In this chapter, however, I dig a little deeper into stocks, so for some people, this could be a bit more challenging.

Learning how to analyze stocks is a useful skill to know. After all, just because you discovered a good-looking stock doesn't mean it's a smart idea to buy it now. In fact, once you've found a stock, there are several ways to determine whether it's worth holding or buying. The two main methods for analyzing stocks are *fundamental analysis* and *technical analysis*.

I give an overview to both approaches, which can quickly help you to determine whether a stock is a smart purchase. Then I show how to use these analytical tools to make buy and sell decisions. Fortunately, you don't have to be an expert to use these methods. Nevertheless, although these tools are easy to use, it still takes time to learn how to use them properly.

Unfortunately, many people simply buy stocks because a friend or neighbor or a random person on Instagram or YouTube, recommended it.

Some investors don't do their homework. They just buy. That is usually not a good idea.

OVERVIEW OF FUNDAMENTAL ANALYSIS

Many long-term investors use *fundamental analysis* because their objective is to buy a good stock at a reasonable price. If their analysis is correct, these investors should be rewarded with a higher stock price. If their analysis is wrong, however, they may be punished with a lower stock price.

By using fundamental analysis, investors discover everything they can about the health of the company behind the stock. Most important, they must determine if the company's earnings will increase in the future. Admittedly, this method takes time because it means doing research.

For example, investors look at how much the company earns, how large their debt is, and who is managing the company. All of this information and more can be found on the company's *balance sheet*.

Another place to find information is in the company's *annual report*, which can be found online. This report may not be exciting to read, but it contains important financial documents, including the balance sheet and *income statement*. It also includes a discussion of marketing and advertising strategies.

WHAT FUNDAMENTAL ANALYSTS WANT TO KNOW

There is certain information about the company that fundamental analysts want to know. Here is a brief list of what they look at:

- Earnings per share (EPS):

    One of the most important pieces of information is the company's EPS. You may love the company and buy its products, but if the business isn't consistently growing its profits (i.e., increasing earnings) by enough to satisfy Wall Street, its stock price will eventually fall.

    Sometimes there are exceptions. For example, a stock may currently not be earning any money, but its stock price can still increase. Perhaps it has a business model that investors love. For example, when Amazon was a young company, it lost money each of its first 14 years, but the stock price still climbed higher. Those investors who had high hopes for the company's future were richly rewarded when Amazon became an extremely successful company.

    Therefore, when deciding whether to buy or keep a stock, always look at EPS (displayed on financial websites and at the *stock snapshot* page, discussed later in this chapter).

- The price/earnings ratio (P/E):

    Many investors like to use the P/E ratio to determine when a stock is selling for a reasonable price. To be precise, the P/E ratio is the stock price divided by the EPS. Investors can use the P/E ratio to quickly compare a company with its competitors.

    In general, companies with a low P/E stock tend to be growing earnings slowly. A low P/E may also mean that a company's stock is low when compared to its earnings. These stocks are attractive to investors looking for a bargain.

    A high P/E ratio may mean that a company's stock is high when compared to its earnings. Investors expect stocks with a high P/E to be growing earnings quickly and have the potential for spectacular growth.

    Value investors, or those looking for stocks that are on sale, prefer to buy dividend-paying stocks with a low P/E ratio. Growth investors, however, are willing to "pay up" for stocks that have the potential to grow in the future. These investors will buy stocks with a high P/E ratio.

- Company information:

   A fundamental analyst does research. They look at qualitative information such as whether the company is in a thriving industry. They also want the company to be a leader in that industry.

   Fundamental analysts also look at the company's competitors to see how well they are doing. Finally, as mentioned previously, fundamental analysts spend a lot of time studying the balance sheet and income statement. This is where they find out the truth about how much income, or debt, the company has.

PSYCHOLOGY UNDERMINES THE FUNDAMENTALS

Here's something that is annoying but true: sometimes fundamental analysts determine that a company is an excellent buy, and yet, the stock price declines!

This happens a lot in the stock market. The reason is because of something else: psychology. Even when investors buy stock in a great company, because of emotional reasons, a lot of other people may sell the stock (e.g., there are more sellers than buyers), and the price drops.

Here's an example: Let's say you own stock in a solid bank with good fundamentals. Then one day, a different bank reports that it is losing money and customers. As expected, the stock price plunges.

Guess what happens next? Traders and investors who own stock in *other* banks begin to sell. They sell stock in the good banks and also sell stock in the bad banks—they don't care. They sell without thinking. This means that even though you may own a stock in a healthy bank, the price may fall that day, and perhaps for even longer.

The reason is simple. When people get overly emotional about a stock, either too greedy or fearful, they will buy or sell not because of a company's earnings but based on their emotions.

OVERVIEW OF TECHNICAL ANALYSIS

Technical analysis is a method used to evaluate the market or a stock's direction. Although used mostly by traders to give clues to short-term market direction, long-term investors can also use technical analysis before buying any stock.

The funny thing about technical analysis is that it's usually not that technical. In fact, some of the most useful technical indicators for beginners are easy to use and understand. In this section, I give a brief introduction.

One of the main purposes of technical analysis is to quickly determine when to enter or exit a stock position. It can also give an overview of the entire stock market, along with clues as to which direction it may be headed.

Keep in mind that technical analysis is not the Holy Grail. The tools listed next are guides rather than the final word. These indicators give clues as to what the stock market or a stock is doing. Think of technical analysis as one piece of a larger puzzle called the stock market. Sometimes these clues are helpful and at other times they provide false or useless signals.

The Stock Chart

When using technical analysis, you can get clues about a stock's direction by looking at a *stock chart*. The stock chart is loaded with useful information such as whether a stock is *overbought* or *oversold*, whether the stock *trend* is moving higher or lower, and how many shares are trading (i.e., *volume*).

Figure 9.1 Stock Chart

SOURCE: Adapted from Yahoo Finance.

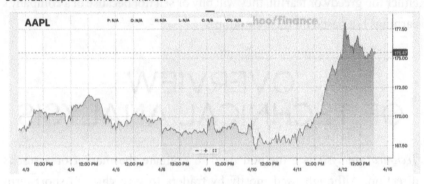

The best way to explain technical analysis is with a chart. You can find a stock chart by logging onto your brokerage account and entering a stock symbol. There are also dozens of websites with stock charts, including Stockcharts, Barchart, *Barron's*, Bloomberg, Briefing, CNBC, CNN Business, *Financial Times*, Google Finance, Kiplinger, MarketWatch, MSN Money, *Wall Street Journal*, and Yahoo Finance, to name a few.

Figure 9.1 shows a five-day stock chart of Apple Computer. After a flat start, Apple stock zoomed higher later in the week, delighting investors.

> Note: Most stock charts are set to a three-month *time frame*.

Uptrends and Downtrends

In Figure 9.1, the stock's *trend* is displayed. A trend is simply the direction of the stock price, either up, down, or sideways. The figure also shows that Apple was in a sideways trend for several days when it broke out into a strong *uptrend*, which is when the price trend is moving higher, a positive signal.

However, when the price has been moving lower, that is typically a negative signal for the stock. It is called a *downtrend*. If a stock you own continues to fall over a long time period (and you can see the price line dropping on a stock chart), you may not want to buy additional shares. In this example, perhaps it's not a good time to buy until the downtrend ends and the stock begins to rally.

Although stock prices move up and down, there are also times when the stock moves in the same direction for an extended period. This is called a *sideways* trend. Looking at Figure 9.1, you can see that Apple was in a sideways trend for several days.

During a sideways trend, it is usually difficult to make a profit. The best advice for long-term investors is to stay disciplined and continue your periodic investing. No one ever knows when the sideways trend will end, so it's best to hold your position.

One great thing about a stock chart is that uptrends, downtrends, and sideways trends can easily be seen without having to do any math.

Moving Averages

On a stock chart, you can see three multicolored lines (they will look black and gray in a book). Those lines represent the 50-day, 100-day, and 200-day moving averages. Basically, when the stock price on a chart is above all three moving averages, that is bullish (i.e., positive). The stock is likely in an uptrend.

However, when the stock price is below the three moving averages, that is usually bearish (i.e., negative). Although stock prices do reverse direction, it's not a good sign when a stock is below its three moving averages. The stock is likely in a downtrend.

Before investing in a stock, look at the moving averages on a stock chart. If the stock has recently moved above its moving averages, it may be a buy signal. If the stock is below its moving averages, many traders wait before buying the stock.

After all, a falling stock may keep going lower and lower. However, if a stock is moving sideways, many traders wait for an uptrend to begin before making a purchase.

> Hint to traders: No matter how much you love the company or its products, if the stock is moving lower, if the stock trend is down, and if the stock is below its three moving averages, you should look for another stock to buy—at least for now.

Volume

The volume bars are located at the bottom of the stock chart. These bars display the number of shares traded throughout the day. Volume is important to traders because it tells them how many other traders are buying and selling.

Many traders use volume to help with trading decisions. Typically, it is bullish when stocks move higher on higher volume.

Many traders prefer to buy stocks that have a lot of volume and liquidity, and that means buying well-known stocks that many other investors buy or sell every day. Using this approach means avoiding stocks with low volume. Low-volume stocks may be harder to sell in the future.

THE WATCH LIST

While thinking of stocks to buy, you may want to create a "watch list" at your brokerage firm's website (nearly every broker has one). A watch list is a list of stocks that you are interested in following or buying. As you think of stock ideas, enter them in your watch list.

All of the basic information about the stock is displayed. This includes important facts such as the stock price, the *bid-ask price*, volume, and the 52-week high and low prices.

THE STOCK SNAPSHOT PAGE

One day you may find a stock you really want to buy. That is when you will go to the *stock snapshot* page, which gives a quick overview of the company and stock. Sometimes the snapshot page is listed on a "research" or "statistics" tab, and other times it is on the first page of the brokerage screen.

When you find the stock snapshot page, enter any *stock symbol* that you want. All of the important data about the company and its stock will be displayed.

Every brokerage firm has a stock snapshot page, including print and online sites mentioned throughout the book. (A full list of useful financial websites is in the Appendix.)

If you haven't signed up with a brokerage firm yet, type the stock symbol followed by "stock snapshot page" in a search engine. Many websites will appear with data about the stock.

Figure 9.2 shows a sample stock snapshot (or statistics) page, which displays a lot of important information about a stock.

The first piece of data on the snapshot page is fundamental data such as quarterly and yearly revenue, and gross profits. It also includes technical data such as a stock's 52-week high or low, volume, and its moving averages.

The stock or ETF's bid and ask price (i.e., the stock quote) will be displayed at the top of page. Stock prices constantly change during the day. However, if you are checking a mutual fund, you'd only see the final price (i.e., NAV) from the previous day's market close.

Figure 9.2 Stock Snapshot or Statistics Page

SOURCE: Adapted from Yahoo Finance.

Financial Highlights		Trading Information	
Fiscal Year		**Stock Price History**	
Fiscal Year Ends	9/30/2023	Beta (5Y Monthly)	1.28
Most Recent Quarter (mrq)	12/30/2023	52 Week Range	5.95%
Profitability		S&P 500 52-Week Change	25.65%
Profit Margin	26.16%	52 Week High	199.62
Operating Margin (ttm)	33.76%	52 Week Low	162.80
Management Effectiveness		50-Day Moving Average	177.23
Return on Assets (ttm)	21.18%	200-Day Moving Average	182.83
Return on Equity (ttm)	154.27%	**Share Statistics**	
Income Statement		Avg Vol (3 month)	61.11M
Revenue (ttm)	385.71B	Avg Vol (10 day)	52.51M
Revenue Per Share (ttm)	24.65	Shares Outstanding	15.44B
Quarterly Revenue Growth (yoy)	2.10%	Implied Shares Outstanding	15.44B
Gross Profit (ttm)	--	Float	15.41B

CONCLUSION

Now that you have a better idea of how to analyze stocks, in the next chapter, I walk you through the buying and selling process. Although I'm certain you and your child can figure out how to buy and sell stocks on your own, for your convenience, in Chapter 10, I list the steps. I also introduce a few buying and selling strategies that may be helpful.

CHAPTER TEN
BUYING AND SELLING

The brokerage firms have made it extremely easy to buy and sell stocks. In case you've never done it before, I list the steps in the first sidebar. Later, I will discuss a number of buying and selling strategies, which I believe you'll find useful, even if it can get a little technical at times.

BUYING STOCKS

Just in case buying stocks is a new experience for you, following are the instructions for buying a stock. The steps are the same if buying an ETF.

How to Buy a Stock (or ETF)

Step 1: Enter your User ID and password to login to your account. The first screen is an account overview, including account balance and a position (if any).

Step 2 (Buy button): On the front page, find the "Stocks" tab. Then find the "Buy" button and press it. (Some brokerage firms may have a dropdown menu with "Trade" or "Action" tabs rather than a Buy button.) The Buy Order screen appears.

Step 3 (Stock symbol): Enter the stock symbol. Always double-check to be certain you enter the correct symbol.

Step 4 (Quantity): Select how many shares you want to buy (a minimum of one share).

Step 5 (Order type): You must choose a *limit order* or *market order*. A market order is filled (i.e., executed) immediately at the ask price, but it may not be the best price for you. However, a limit order allows you to select the highest price you are willing to pay. With a limit order, you are allowed to negotiate the price, but it usually takes more time to get it filled.

Note: Although it may take a few seconds longer, a limit order is a better choice because you may get a lower price. If you're in a hurry, and prefer not to negotiate, then a market order is acceptable.

Analogy: When going to a car dealership to buy a car, you can see the difference between a limit order and a market order. You can pay the dealer's sticker price (i.e., market order) and get the car immediately. You can also negotiate for a better price (i.e., limit order), but the dealer may choose not to accept your limit price and make a counter offer, thereby lowering their limit price.

Step 6 (Bid or ask price): When entering a limit order, the computer screen displays a *bid price* (the highest published price anyone is willing to accept) and the *ask price* (the lowest price anyone is offering to pay). This is also known as the *stock quote*. Think of the bid and ask price as auction prices. If possible, try to buy at a price that is between the bid and ask price.

Step 7 (Payment screen): When finished, the computer calculates the total cost. Verify that this is the correct amount.

Stock Market Math

Some people are nervous about mathematics. Fortunately, when buying or selling stocks, the math is very basic. Let's go over a couple of examples, which should help you understand how it's done.

Example 1: Let's say you want to buy 100 shares of the stock, YYYY, which last traded for $15 per share. To buy this stock at $15 per share, it will cost $1,500 ($15 per share × 100 shares). After pressing the Enter key, $1,500 will be transferred from your cash account. You now own 100 shares of YYYY.

Calculating profit or loss: Here's the important part. Because you bought 100 shares of YYYY, every time that YYYY moves higher by one *point* (e.g., from $15 to $16), your gain is $100 ($1 per share × 100 shares). However, when YYYY moves lower by one point, you lose $100.

Reminder: When a stock price goes higher or lower, Wall Street uses the word *point* to describe the price change. Therefore, if a stock you own moves from $52 per share to $53 per share, they will say it went up by 1 point. And if your stock dropped from $52 to $49 per share, they say it fell by 3 points.

Buy-and-hold investors plan to hold their 100 shares, perhaps buying more shares over time. In the previous example, traders will sell at $17 per share and be happy with a $200 gain. For most people, it makes sense to buy a stock and hold it for longer, looking for even larger gains.

Example 2: Let's say that the price of YYYY rises by 5 points over the next month. Because you own 100 shares, you earned a profit of $500 (100 shares × $5). For every point that YYYY moves up, you make $100. That's how you build wealth in the stock market.

Unfortunately, there are no guarantees that the shares you own will keep moving higher, but if you choose a winner, you should be very happy with the results.

Note: If you are teaching your child about buying and selling stocks, you may want to use these examples to explain. When buying an ETF, the steps are identical. With a mutual fund, almost no math is involved. When buying a mutual fund, on the brokerage screen, type how much money you want to invest and the computer does the rest. When selling a mutual fund, you enter how many shares to sell into the computer and the order is filled at the next NAV.

After Buying Stock

It's an exciting feeling to buy your first stock. If you choose the right stock at the right time, you'll make a profit. If you're a long-term investor, you don't have to do much other than monitoring the stock every few weeks or months.

STOCK-BUYING STRATEGIES

Now that you know how to buy stocks, let's discuss two stock-buying strategies, one that is new, *scaling*, and the other that is an old favorite, dollar cost averaging. You can use either of these strategies when buying stocks.

Buying Strategy 1: Scale into an Investment

Scaling into a stock means buying only a few shares at a time rather making one large investment (i.e., lump sum). *Scaling* into a stock is a buying strategy that enables you to gradually accumulate shares rather than dumping a lot of money into a single stock at one time.

There usually is no need to rush into buying a large number of shares at one time. Almost any stock you want to buy will be there in the next hour, the next day, and the next week. Scaling into an investment takes more patience, but it is a less risky buying method.

For example, let's say there is a stock you want to buy. Instead of investing $100 at one time, consider first buying $25 worth in the first transaction. In other words, stagger the purchase over a short or long time period using only a small portion of your money each time.

After the first investment, monitor the stock's performance. Decide whether to buy more shares. If the stock price doesn't budge, or falls, consider waiting before adding to the position. If the stock keeps dropping, wait until it stops moving lower, and rises again, before buying more shares.

However, if the stock price rises instead of falls, it's okay to make another purchase. With scaling, the idea is to make regular investments until the entire amount has been invested.

> Note: Not everyone is a fan of scaling. If you have a large sum of money that is burning a hole in your pocket, then by all means invest the entire amount. Scaling into an investment is a risk-reducing suggestion, and is not a rule.

Buying Strategy 2: Dollar Cost Averaging

I've previously discussed dollar cost averaging when buying index funds. However, you can also dollar cost average with individual stocks. Here's an example of how it works with stocks.

Let's say you invest $200 in XYZ when it's at $20 per share. During the next month, XYZ falls to $18 per share, and you invest another $200. A month later, XYZ rises to $22 per share, and you invest another $200. Investing the same $200 every month is dollar cost averaging.

By buying shares at different prices, over time you probably own more shares but at higher prices. This method is mathematically preferable to the lump-sum investing method, in which investors buy a lot of shares at one time. Even if XYZ experienced temporary pullbacks, dollar cost averaging works. Actually, it works even better during down markets as you are buying more shares at lower prices.

Note: The difference between dollar cost averaging and scaling into an investment is this: with dollar cost averaging, you invest the same amount of money every month (or choose another time period). With scaling, you invest any amount whenever you want to invest.

SELLING STOCKS

If you are new to the stock market and want to know the exact steps required to sell a stock (or ETF), the following sidebar should meet your needs. After the sidebar, I discuss a few useful selling strategies.

How to Sell a Stock (Step-by-Step)

The mechanics of selling a stock is relatively easy (although figuring out *when* to sell is a challenge). The following directions are for anyone who needs step-by-step instructions. (In reality, these steps are nearly the same as when buying.)

Step 1: Go to your brokerage website and select the stock order screen.

Step 2: Enter the correct stock symbol in the symbol box.

Step 3: Choose "Sell Order" from the drop-down menu (your screen may have a different label such as "Sell" or "Trade").

(Continued)

Step 4: Type in the number of shares you want to sell.

Step 5: Select "Limit order" from the drop-down menu. As you recall, you can enter a limit or market order. I recommend a limit order because it gives investors more control over the selling price. A market order is used only when you must sell the stock RIGHT NOW.

Step 6: The bid and ask prices (i.e., the quote) will be displayed, for example, $34.33 × $34.43. When selling with a limit order, you typically sell at or near the bid price (i.e., the lower price). By selling near the bid price, you increase the likelihood that your stock is sold in a timely matter.

Step 7: Enter all of the required information on the screen and press the "Sell" button. The computer calculates exactly how much cash you'll receive if the order you entered is executed.

Step 8: If the order is filled (i.e., executed), the money from the sale is transferred to your cash account.

Step 9: There is a one-day settlement (not including Saturday and Sunday). The cash from the sale is delivered to your account one day after the trade. Note: Trades used to be settled in two days but the rule was changed in 2024.

WHEN TO SELL STOCK

As you know, this book is focused on investing in index funds and stocks and holding for the long term. The idea is to buy and hold while selling as little as possible. Nevertheless, there will be times when you want or need to sell stock.

Perhaps the company is going through a rough period, or they have too much debt, or the stock price is falling. Maybe you found a stock with better prospects, or the stock has not performed as well as you hoped. Whatever the reason, it may be a good time to sell.

If you can sell stock for a gain, that's great. Other times, you may have to sell the stock at a loss, and that's okay if you are selling to avoid even bigger losses. As mentioned previously, one of the most important trading rules is "Cut your losses."

STOCK SELLING STRATEGIES

Let's discuss a number of selling strategies using fundamental and technical analysis. (If you need a refresher course, return to Chapter 9 for an overview of fundamental and technical analysis.)

Selling Strategy: Sell Using Fundamental Analysis

Many investors use fundamental analysis to help decide when to sell. Here are five fundamental reasons why you may want to sell a stock.

- Consider selling when a company's earnings weaken, debt is too high, or if costs have increased. You may have to do some detective work but most of this information can be found on the balance sheet and income statement. The hard part is confirming that the company is in trouble before the price tumbles. This information is not always easy to uncover. It took Sears nearly a decade of slowing growth and poor earnings before it finally went out of business. Nevertheless, the clues were telling a story that the company was struggling, but only if investors were willing to look.

- Be on guard for negative news about the company. The challenge is identifying when the bad news is so bad that it will affect the stock price. As mentioned previously, after Steve Jobs left Apple in 1985, Apple's stock price plunged to pennies per share (split-adjusted price). At that time, Apple nearly went bankrupt when Jobs' successor was unable to keep the magic going. It was only after Jobs came back that Apple returned to greatness, and its stock price recovered. It was not easy to determine at that time whether Apple was a buy or a sell. Many investors guessed wrong.

- Consider selling when a company cuts its dividend. When GE cut their dividend from 12 cents per share to 1 cent per share, that was a huge red flag. Smart investors sold their shares.

- Consider selling if a company fires their CEO. Sometimes a CEO change is a good move, and sometimes not. If there is a major management change, pay close attention to the reasons why. Is it because the previous CEO did a poor job? If you have the time, find out everything you can about the new CEO by reading news articles. If the former CEO just retired, there is no reason for concern.

- If you visit a store in person or online, see whether the store is crowded with customers holding shopping bags, if you like the products they are selling, and if the store is clean and well-managed. Before a company loses money and goes out of business, there are many clues. For example, employees are not interested in helping customers, the store is dirty or disorganized, and there are few customers shopping during peak hours or at holidays.

Selling Strategy: Sell Using Technical Analysis

Selling your shares using technical analysis is a different animal. To decide when to sell, look at a stock chart for clues. Consider selling a stock when the stock price falls below its 50-day moving average. If it's also below its 100- and 200-day moving averages, that stock may be in trouble. Monitor the position closely. If there are no signs of a recovery, this stock may need to be sold.

As a long-term investor, the most important moving average is the almighty 200-day moving average. Once a stock falls below the 200-day moving average, it is in a long-term downtrend, and it may be time to think about selling some shares. Exception: If you are using the dollar cost averaging strategy, you may ignore moving averages and continue adding to your position each month.

> Hint: Long-term investors rely more on fundamental analysis than technical analysis. However, it still makes sense to watch the 200-day moving average. Once a stock falls below its 200-day moving average, think about cutting losses and selling. This is a decision only you can make.

Here is one more selling strategy that a number of investors use.

Selling Strategy: Sell in Quarters and Halves

If you've made a ton of money on a stock or other investment and aren't sure when to sell, consider selling one half or one quarter of the investment.

If the stock keeps moving higher, consider selling another quarter or half. Selling in portions is one way to lock in profits while continuing to participate in additional rallies. As you probably guessed, with this strategy you are "scaling out" of a position.

> Note: Although scaling out of a position makes sense, there may be times you need to cut your losses, or, hopefully, lock in large profits. In these examples, instead of scaling out, just sell the entire position.

Selling Summary

To review, find a magnificent company that makes fantastic products, and buy its stock if the shares are available at a reasonable price. If the company pays dividends, that's even better. Each month, buy additional shares of stock.

As long as the company has met your expectations, and people are buying its products, hold the stock and don't sell. That's it!

> Note: Usually there are a lot of clues and indicators that help with the selling decision. If you want all of the fundamental and technical reasons for buying or selling a stock, including additional strategies, feel free to read my previous book, *Understanding Stocks*.

CONCLUSION

Now that you know how to buy and sell stocks, in Chapter 11, I'll discuss one of the most difficult aspects of investing: controlling emotions. The mechanics of buying and selling stocks can be taught. The hard part for most people is having the discipline and self-control to manage their investments.

CHAPTER ELEVEN
TRAPS AND PITFALLS

I t's not easy to teach new investors about the psychological traps and pitfalls that await them when entering the stock market. Nevertheless, in this chapter I do my best to write about the emotional challenges that investors face nearly every day.

Many investors begin with a positive attitude and high hopes of making some money. Some even dream of earning a fortune. Others believe they can wish their way to riches. My job—one I take seriously—is to describe what to expect when entering the dangerous waters of a shark-infested stock market.

People tend to believe that the stock market is predictable and sane, but in reality, the market behaves like a bipolar acquaintance who jumps from one emotion to another. Sure, the market can go for months with no unusual flareups, and then for no reason at all, it acts irrationally. The pros call this volatility.

I wrote this chapter to help you avoid errors that will cost money. I'm an expert on making mistakes; I have personally made every mistake included in this chapter.

Fortunately, being an investor is a lot easier and not as emotionally draining as being a trader. Buying index funds is even less stressful.

The contents of this chapter should be helpful, especially if you are new to the stock market. It is also a good idea to review the potential pitfalls and traps each year to make sure you are not making money-losing mistakes. After all, you are not in the market to lose money. If you are unsatisfied with your investment returns, read this chapter thoroughly to see if you can identify any problems.

INVESTOR QUOTES

The following subsections provide a flawed investor quote followed by a brief suggestion.

"I Play It by Ear."

Suggestion: Playing it by ear is risky business. It means there are no strategies, rules, goals, or plans. Anyone who plays it by ear in the market will eventually lose money when their luck runs out. Instead of "winging it," they should create an investment plan, design a strategy, and follow a few basic rules.

"I Can't Be Wrong!"

Suggestion: Most people hate to admit they're wrong. That's why they will hold their beloved losers far too long, unwilling to admit defeat. Even worse, some investors back up their overconfidence by betting even more money on a "can't lose" stock. That's not investing—it's gambling. Overconfidence in the stock market often leads to lost money. Remember this: The only one who is never wrong about the market is the market itself. The best idea is to enter the market with a hopeful but realistic attitude. And, yes, investors can be, and often are, wrong.

"It's So Easy to Make Money in the Stock Market."

Suggestion: This mistake has cost many smart people tons of cash. They enter the market thinking it's easy to make money. Instead, they lose, which they blame on everyone but themselves. It's fine to enter the market with a positive attitude, but be humble. The market is smarter than everyone, so either follow it, get out of its way, or find a strategy that beats it.

"I Don't Have the Money to Invest Right Now."

Suggestion: Not investing in the stock market is one of the biggest mistakes of all. Instead of making excuses of why they can't afford to invest, people should open an account with whatever they can afford. Recognize the power of starting early and add small sums when possible. In other words, they should start small, then gradually increase the amount invested. Bottom line: It's not important how much money is invested, only that they get started.

"I Don't Know When to Sell."

Suggestion: Knowing when to sell a stock can be challenging. Many investors sell too early or too late, and some never sell at all. Buying an index fund solves a lot of the selling problems because it may be held indefinitely. Investors should sell a stock when it is moving in the wrong direction or they are losing too much money. It's also smart to sell some shares when the market has gone up too high and too fast. They can use technical or fundamental analysis to help with the selling decision.

"My Stock Will Come Back to Even."

Suggestion: Investors who hold onto losing stocks for too long tell themselves that their stock will eventually return to the price they paid for it. Sometimes they are right, but losing stocks often keep losing. If the stock doesn't come back to even anytime soon, they should stop the bleeding and sell. Cutting losses is one of the smartest moves an investor can make when holding a dud. There are plenty of other fish in the stock market sea.

"This Is Fun! I Love Buying Stocks."

Suggestion: If buying stocks feels like a fun game, it's a red flag. Buying stocks is not a game nor should it be done for entertainment. When it feels that way, investors may have accidentally crossed over to the gambling side. Another red flag is when investors trade too many stocks at one time or bet too much money. Unless they are professionals, that is speculating, not investing.

"I Love My Stock but It Keeps Falling."

Suggestion: Although it's wonderful to believe in a company and cheer its success, investors who fall in love with their stocks are unable to view it objectively. If they are overly loyal to the company and refuse to let go even as it's sinking, they could lose even more money. Loyal investors who bought and held shares of Sears, Lehman Brothers, WorldCom, and tons of other stocks didn't sell their darlings until it was way too late. One question investors should ask themselves is, Why do you still love the stock when it has betrayed you?

"I Hate Losing Money on This Stock but I Don't Want to Sell. What Should I Do?"

Suggestion: If holding a losing stock that's not coming out of the basement anytime soon, think about selling. In the stock market and in life, when things aren't working out, even after patiently waiting, sometimes the best move is cut your losses. If investors are holding a stock that keeps falling, it's smart to analyze whether it's worth holding. Sell confirmed losers and move on.

"If I Don't Buy This Stock by Friday, I'll Never Get the Chance Again!"

Suggestion: This is such a common ailment that there is a nickname, FOMO, or the fear of missing out. This is the fear that causes people to get scammed, invest too much money in a junk stock, or buy worthless items just because they are on sale. It's the fear that if they don't act RIGHT NOW, they will miss out on the investment of the century. Rarely is there a need to buy a stock immediately. To avoid getting fooled into buying a stock (or anything else) immediately, think it through, and wait until the next day. FOMO has caused many smart people to act really dumb.

"I Can't Help Myself. I Buy More Shares When the Market Is Higher and I Sell When It's Lower."

Suggestion: Fear and greed have doomed many investors. Fear causes investors to sell too early or at the bottom, and greed causes them to buy at the top. If the market appears to be at extremes, either moving much lower or moving too high, it's a good time to use technical analysis to decide whether to hold, sell, or buy rather than relying on emotions.

Red flag: Being overly emotional about money and investments is one reason why so many people make bad financial decisions. Getting giddy and giving high fives when making money or throwing phones or office chairs when losing money is a red flag that trouble is coming. Keep those emotions under control.

"I'm Afraid I'll Lose All of My Money. I'm Going to Sell Everything!"

Suggestion: This happens a lot. Emotional investors want to sell all their stocks whenever the market makes a huge drop, usually at the bottom. Instead, they should take a deep breath and relax. Use technical analysis to identify if the market is *oversold*. If this is confirmed, instead of panic selling, they should either hold or even add to their position. As I wrote in the Introduction, this is the opposite of what most investors do!

Another idea for nervous investors is to occasionally move a little money into fixed income products (but try to do this before the market plunges). They may not make much money in fixed income, but they'll get a good night's sleep.

"My Neighbor Told Me to Buy (Fill-in-the-Blank). He Said It Will Be the Next Amazon."

Suggestion: Sure, we all want to make fast money, but stock tips rarely come from neighbors, a stranger on TV, or on social media. More than likely, their tips are worthless. Also, if investors don't understand what they are buying, they shouldn't buy. If possible, ask the tipster why they think the stock is so great. If there are any doubts about the answers, they should do their own research and find their own stocks.

"Everyone Is Talking About (Fill-in-the-Blank). Should I Buy It?"

Suggestion: It's very tempting to make large, risky bets with hot stocks that "everyone" is talking about. Usually, it's already too late to profit. Instead, investors should make smaller, less-risky investments in well-known stocks that are not as exciting but which should give excellent returns over a long time period.

"My Friend Told Me He Is Making Big Money Day-Trading Stocks. Should I Do It?"

Suggestion: The short answer is no. Day trading is an incredibly difficult strategy with which only a few succeed. Typically, they are seasoned professional traders with years of training and access to huge sums of money. Amateurs such as your friend who trade, stocks and options almost always lose money over time. Often, these traders brag about the days they make money but don't talk about the times they lose. The best advice is not to day trade, and don't follow people who do. More likely than not, they are gambling, not trading.

"I Just Made a Fortune from (Fill-in-the-Blank)! What Should I Do?"

Suggestion: Getting a lot of money at one time is like a sugar high that may cause rational people to act irrational. When receiving a large lump-sum payment such as an inheritance, a paycheck with a bonus, or from the stock market, at first it's wise to put the money into a cash account. Then for the next three to six months, plan, organize, and dream, but don't make any impulsive financial moves. It's almost always a mistake to make important financial decisions when feeling fear, greed, sadness, and especially euphoria. If the money is especially large, consider hiring a financial advisor for help.

"I Went on Margin to Buy This Stock. I'm Praying It Will Go Higher."

Suggestion: Margin enables investors to borrow money from the brokerage to buy more stock. Investors pay interest on the borrowed funds, plus they're on the hook for big bucks if the stock price tumbles. Investors who use margin feel double the pain when the stock price goes in the wrong direction. Advice to most investors: Don't go on margin!

"My Friend Said the Market Is Going to Crash! I'm Thinking of Selling Everything!"

Suggestion: Many people like to scare others by predicting that a crash is coming soon. It's best to ignore them. The facts: Every few years, there is a major stock market decline, or more often, a 10% correction. If holding an index fund, it's best if investors stay the course. Continue with your monthly investment and dollar cost averaging strategy. Let other people lose their heads and money when they abandon the indexing strategy and panic. In addition, if you own individual stocks, don't sell in a panic. If anything, buy high-quality stocks when they are on sale.

"I Need to Get Rich Fast. What Stock Should I Buy?"

Suggestion: The stock market is not a fairy godmother who makes financial problems disappear. Wealth can be achieved, but it almost never happens quickly. Stick to the sound strategies included in this book and don't try to get rich fast. In addition, trying to get rich fast with investments such as penny stocks or worthless cryptocurrencies (or SPACs, memes, and NFTs) is too risky. Those who get in and out early may make money, but those late to the game stand little chance of winning. Like any fad, what comes up must come down, and that's when paper millionaires get wiped out.

"I Was Told to Buy Low and Sell High. How Do I Do That?"

Suggestion: Trying to get in at the bottom or sell at the top is market timing, and is a nearly impossible goal. Although the cute saying, "Buy low, sell high," has been around for decades, in reality, very few traders get it right. When anyone says you should buy low and sell high, you can quote the great investor Bernard Baruch, who said, "Don't try to buy at the bottom and sell at the top. It can't be done—except by liars." A much more realistic plan is to invest now and sell years later at a higher price.

"I Just Made $1,000 on My Index Fund. I Am Going to Sell It Tomorrow and Lock in the Profit."

Suggestion: Many investors abandon their long-term plans by selling too early. Perhaps they needed the money or they were afraid to lose their profits. Whatever the reason, they changed from a long-term investor to a short-term trader. The solution: Investors should stick with their long-term plan and hold onto their investments until there is a reason to sell. Making a profit is not enough reason to sell.

"I Have to Sell My Index Fund Now. I Need the Money."

Suggestion: Although many investors plan to hold their index fund forever, emergencies can get in the way. It happens. Unfortunately, if they sell an index fund early, that money is probably not coming back. Here's a solution: Don't sell! (The exception is if their children own an index fund in a 529 plan that is sold to pay for educational expenses.)

"My Child Turned 18 and Told Me They're Going to Sell Their Index Fund."

Suggestion: Parents can try to give their children a financial education, but when they turn 18, they become legal adults. Even though they shouldn't blow their index money on stupid stuff, some will. With any luck, they will learn from their mistakes, get a job, and create a new investment account with a 401(k) at their new job. Then they can start all over again using the investment strategies they learned from you and this book.

How I Got Scammed

I've often said that I write books to help others avoid the dumb mistakes I've made as an investor and trader. Here's one of my early mistakes, a lesson I hope you learn from.

Early in my career, I accumulated a large sum of money investing in index funds and mutual funds through a 401(k) at work. I decided to use some of that excess cash to buy individual stocks. I ran into a knowledgeable acquaintance who recommended buying stock in a cell phone company located in Texas. It was trading around $15 per share. My acquaintance predicted that it would go to $30 per share within months.

I was eager to buy 2,000 shares at $15 per share for a total cost of $30,000. I would make $2,000 every time the stock price rose by one point. I was excited by how much money I "could" make.

I was so sure about the stock I opened a *margin* account to buy another 2,000 shares (in other words, I borrowed $30,000 from the brokerage firm to buy 2,000 additional shares). Because I now owned 4,000 shares, I would earn a paper gain of $4,000 per point. Wow!

Perhaps the most amazing thing was that my acquaintance was right. Within four months, the stock actually did make it to $30 per share, giving me an unrealized gain of $60,000.

I called my acquaintance for advice. Should I hold on for bigger profits, or sell? He told me the stock was going even higher, and that I should not sell. Because he had been right about the stock, I followed his advice, thereby changing my original investment plan. Big mistake.

I'll never forget the day when I received my first, and last, *margin call*. The broker called before the market opened to say that, during the night, this phone company stock had plunged from $32 per share to less than $4 per share. The broker told me I had to come up with the cash immediately. How was this possible?

The broker told me I could meet the margin call by investing another $30,000, or I could sell the stock for $4 per share and take a huge loss.

I didn't want to add money to a losing position (that was the smartest decision I ever made), so I told the broker to sell the entire position at the market open. Once the stock was sold, I was shocked when I looked at my brokerage statement: I had lost $22,000 of my own money plus another $22,000 that I had borrowed from the broker. In other words, I went from a $68,000 gain to a $44,000 loss … in one night.

Later, I found out the stock I had bought was part of a "pump-and-dump" scam. My acquaintance and his unethical buddies pumped the stock higher using money from naive investors like me. As soon as the stock reached $30 per share, they dumped their shares and locked in their gains, leaving investors with huge losses.

A pump-and-dump scheme is illegal. The feds eventually arrested my acquaintance and his criminal friends. He received a light sentence for his scam, but it didn't help me. The $44,000 I lost was gone, but I learned a lot of lessons. Eventually, I was able to make back the money with other, sounder investments. However, it took a long time.

I also learned not to listen to tips from anyone, no matter how credible they sounded. Instead, I do my own research and find my own stocks. I also learned how risky it is to use margin. It's similar to buying stocks with a credit card. I also learned that when buying stocks, it's possible to lose big when you choose the wrong stock. I also believe in keeping a healthy supply of cash on the side in case of emergencies.

FAMILY SCAMS

Another lesson I learned the hard way is that when it comes to money, you have to be on guard, even with family members.

I wrote a column for MarketWatch about a close friend, Alan (not his real name), who was scammed out of most of his inheritance, including two houses, by his greedy brother and corrupt sister-in-law. He learned that some siblings betray their own family, even their mother, for a bigger slice of the inheritance pie.

There were a number of red flags that my friend missed, clues that may have helped him avoid being a victim of his greedy sibling. Scammers are not always strangers; sometimes they are family members. Here are some important warning signs:

Red flag: Alan's brother pressured him into signing a contract on the spot. Alan should have refused to be bullied into signing until his own lawyer (or financial advisor) could review it. Because Alan trusted his unethical brother, he signed the documents under the watchful eye of his brother's lawyer. Many scams can be avoided if people would take the time to read documents before signing.

If anyone feels pressured to make a quick decision regarding contracts, investments, or life-changing events, it's best to stop and think. Why not wait a few days? If it involves a contract, let someone else (like a lawyer) read it before signing. Scammers are good at getting others to make fast decisions, too often the wrong ones. Bottom line: Do not make impulsive decisions. Wait before signing anything or making important decisions.

Red Flag: Dishonest family members are secretive and vague. They want to keep you in the dark about their corrupt activities, and will refuse to answer direct questions about what they are doing. They purposely hide relevant information, and make lots of excuses. For example, they may promise to "let you know" or "I'll get back to you later," but never do, hoping you'll forget and move on.

Honest family members, however, explain to other family members what steps they are taking with financial matters, and keep everyone in the loop. They do not distract, deceive, hide, or bully. Honest relatives never make side deals with other family members.

Red flag: It's a red flag when a relative "lawyers up." Some family members may claim they need to "protect" the money while secretly stealing from the estate (this is called a *false flag*). They may even bring in their own unethical lawyers so that they can direct the inheritance money to themselves.

Suggestion: If a family member acts suspiciously, overspends (as executor), or hires unnecessary lawyers, then hire your own lawyer or financial advisor for guidance. Your sibling may discourage you from getting help, or even bully you for seeking outside assistance. Do not back down. Independent counsel is needed to protect yourself and innocent family members.

In Alan's case, his sister-in-law may have been the predator, but his greedy brother went along with the schemes, including pocketing all of the real estate profits.

Red flag: A sibling may suddenly put a wealthy, elderly family member into a nursing home (claiming "they will love it there"), transfer large sums of money out of the estate (which may be impossible to discover until it's too late), or initiate a rushed property sale. All of these actions were taken by my friend's brother and his sister-in-law.

Extremely dishonest folks attempt to change the will to benefit themselves. One of the oldest tricks is to prevent an elderly relative from communicating with others. They may redo the will and force an ill relative to sign, becoming the sole beneficiary.

Some deceitful relatives act as if they don't care about money or a potential inheritance (this is a *red herring*). This lie is created to avoid suspicion. In reality, this person may secretly be planning to take possession of as much family money as possible.

Suggestion: Get involved with your family's financial affairs so you are not left in the dark. Be certain to inform other relatives that you are undertaking this discussion so they do not think of you as the scammer. Be alert to greedy family members who are acting suspiciously, especially when money is involved.

When it comes to family fortunes, be prepared for anything. It's not enough to identify red flags: have the courage to protect what is rightfully yours so you don't become a victim. For example, do not be surprised if unethical family members fight back with bullying tactics and threats—a reason why you must hire independent legal and financial professionals.

Money often brings out greed in people, even those who were previously honest. These people may succumb to the temptation to grab the bulk of the family fortune. For the sake of your financial future and that of other family members, don't allow these fraudsters to get away with a "crime of opportunity." Nip it in the bud by being on guard, verifying all transactions, and, most important, not signing anything unless reviewed by a lawyer.

Unfortunately, once these schemes are uncovered, family relationships will never be the same. It's shameful there are people like Alan's brother and sister-in-law, who are willing to destroy their family just to grab more money for themselves.

CONCLUSION

You may want to review this chapter every year to make sure you're not making any unintended errors. Unfortunately, we often don't recognize our mistakes until the money has already been lost. However, if I could help prevent even one reader from losing money, then writing this chapter will prove its worth.

In Chapter 12, I'll discuss alternative investment products that are a little outside the box. These financial products are not for everyone, but they are there if you, or your children, decide to use them one day.

CHAPTER TWELVE

OUTSIDE-THE-BOX INVESTING

I n this chapter, I discuss alternative investments and strategies, including cryptocurrencies, robo-investing, buying fixed income, DRIPs (dividend reinvestment plans), investing in real estate, and shorting stocks.

This chapter is for those who want to venture beyond the stock world and into different financial products. As always, I try to make it an entertaining read. Perhaps as your child gets older, they will be interested in some of these investment ideas. If so, this chapter will be waiting for them.

Let's begin by discussing one of the most misunderstood investments in recent history: cryptocurrencies.

UNDERSTANDING CRYPTOCURRENCIES

Digital currencies such as cryptocurrencies exploded in popularity a few years ago. After a mysterious birth, a fantastic rise and fall, and another rise, Bitcoin has gone mainstream. They even created a Bitcoin ETF, and more are certain to follow, including crypto index funds.

The two most well-known cryptocurrencies are Bitcoin and Ethereum, but there are thousands more, many with exotic names, and most that are junk. Dozens of new cryptocurrencies are created each week through a complex process called *mining*.

> Hint: If you are going to invest in cryptocurrencies, stick with Bitcoin or Ethereum.

Bitcoin was the first cryptocurrency, one of the reasons it's so well known, rising from $300 per coin to more than $70,000 per coin at one time. You can find the current price of one Bitcoin via an internet search.

Created by a mysterious person, Satoshi Nakamoto (not a real name), cryptocurrency was invented using complicated computer code. Unlike cash, cryptocurrencies cannot be held in your hand. Cryptocurrencies only exist in digital or electronic form.

Even more interesting, crypto is not backed or regulated by any government or financial institution. In a way, it's a bit like the Wild West of currencies. When you buy Bitcoin or another cryptocurrency, the buyer is given a *crypto wallet address*, which is a long, random string of characters. With that address, you may sell the crypto and convert it into US dollars or any other currency. This address allows you to send or receive crypto with other people who use this currency.

Risks of Crypto

The lack of institutional support is the biggest risk of owning crypto. That means if your crypto wallet is hacked or if you send Bitcoin to the wrong person, you can't get your money back. Because crypto exists only as computer code, if you lose your digital wallet, you're out of luck.

Be Careful of Scammers

In addition to these risks, the crypto universe is filled with scammers who try to take your money, or your crypto. Some scammers create fake crypto exchanges, and others insist that you pay them in crypto (suggestion: Never do business with someone who *only* takes crypto as a payment). If you pay a scammer in Bitcoin, you'll never see your money again.

It's also a mistake to do business with an unknown brokerage or crypto exchange. Once in a while, a crypto currency goes bankrupt, and all of the money invested will be gone. This doesn't happen often, but it does mean you should do your due diligence before investing real money into cryptocurrencies. Avoid this disaster by buying crypto only from trustworthy crypto exchanges. You can look up the top exchanges by doing an internet search.

People who must transfer money anonymously (such as criminals or those who live in autocratic countries run by dictators) use cryptocurrencies. Why? Because crypto is nearly impossible to trace. This is also one of the risks of using cryptocurrencies.

Don't Lose Your Crypto Address

If someone loses their crypto address, there isn't much they can do. One hapless man threw away his Bitcoin address, which was stored on his electronic wallet. The address gave him access to millions of dollars in Bitcoin. He begged his home city to allow him access to the city garbage dump. He told them that he planned to hire a professional digger to search for his lost electronic wallet. The city officials refused his request, and the man never saw his electronic wallet again, costing him millions.

Trading Cryptocurrencies

Other people *trade* cryptocurrencies, hoping to buy at a low price and sell at a much higher price. Similar to the traditional currencies market, cryptocurrencies trade 24 hours a day, 7 days a week. It's easy to get hooked on trading them for short-term gains. It's also easy to lose money trading this volatile product.

Risky or Brilliant?

Love them or hate them, crypto isn't going anywhere. Crypto is based on true supply and demand without backing from a central bank. The main problem is that no one knows what the true value of Bitcoin, or any cryptocurrency, is worth. In reality, it's only worth what someone is willing to pay for it at any given moment.

Because crypto is in its infancy, it will take years before this currency is accepted and backed by institutions or governments, if ever. Right now, we don't know whether crypto is a scam, a currency that will be as common as the dollar or euro, or a huge bubble that will pop one day. It could be all three.

Unless you can see the future, it's best to treat this product as a very risky venture. Investing in crypto is like taking a wild rollercoaster ride at a theme park with no seat belts and nothing to hold onto. If you can handle the steep selloffs, extreme volatility, and random price spikes, expect amazing gains and terrible losses, often within one week!

How to Discuss Crypto with Your Child

If an older child decides to invest real money into crypto, start with a small sum. Consider this to be a learning experiment, but not a true financial path to riches. It's fantastic if they make a large gain. However, if all their money is lost, it won't be a life-changing disaster.

Investing with a Robo-Advisor

Although this book is aimed at independent (i.e., self-directed) investors who make their own investing decisions, there is another choice: hire a low-cost *robo-advisor* to make investment decisions. A robo-advisor is an automated financial service that uses computer algorithms to create a diversified portfolio of stocks and funds. The fee for hiring a robo-advisor is less than hiring a money manager. Most brokerage firms give customers the option to use a robo-advisor.

Robo-advisors are popular with investors looking for low-cost investment guidance. In particular, many young people have signed up with robo-advisors, but they are not for everyone. Why not? Because many people prefer to make their own investment decisions, the reason you are reading this book.

Nevertheless, for those who want to know more about this subject, here's an overview.

How to Get Started with a Robo-Advisor

A brokerage firm that uses a robo-advisor requires filling out a questionnaire so they can determine your risk tolerance and investment objectives. Based on the answers, computer algorithms will find investments that match the questionnaire replies. A few brokers with robo-advisors allow customers to speak to a financial advisor, but it may cost more.

Should You Use a Robo-Advisor?

The main advantage of the robo-advisor is the lower cost (when compared to the costs of a human advisor). Only you can decide whether the low cost of robo-advisors are worth the services provided. If you are comfortable managing your own account, buying a low-cost index fund will meet your needs. If not, consider a robo-advisor.

In theory, a good robo-advisor assesses your risk comfort level. Then they devise a plan that has the correct *diversification* and *asset allocation* formulas. The robo-advisor automatically rebalances your portfolio as necessary. In fact, that's what human money managers do, but they charge much higher fees for their services.

One advantage of a robo-advisor is they remain calm when the market is crashing and they don't get giddy when the market is booming. The reason a robo-advisor is always so calm is easy: they are algorithms! Robo-advisors, as you know, don't feel emotions. It's also not their money. When it's your own money on the line, it's easy to get emotional and make mistakes.

Do you really want a robot managing your money? It depends. If you feel you need professional investing help, and are comfortable with an automatic program that devises the so-called ideal portfolio for you at a low cost, then the robo-advisor may be worth trying.

When choosing a robo-advisor, check their fees, the range of investments offered, and how much advice is offered, if any.

Reminder: You can do this on your own for no cost by investing in index funds.

To find a current list of the top robo-advisors, type "rank top robo-advisors" followed by the current year. A list of popular robo-advisors from independent sources will be displayed.

FIXED INCOME INVESTMENTS

Fixed income products are for investors who want to know how much money they will make on an investment, and who don't want to take a lot of risks. These products are especially designed for savers—people who are willing to accept lower returns for a promise to not lose money.

Fixed income products include CDs (certificates of deposit) and cash (which is typically put into a savings or money market account). It also includes bonds, especially US Treasury bonds, notes, and bills. In this section, I discuss various types of bonds. I'll do my best to make the discussion as painless as possible (for most people, the pricing of bonds is a difficult subject).

How Much Can You Earn?

Let's say you buy a CD paying 5% interest over three years. Although the amount of interest earned is relatively small, that doesn't matter much to people who want financial safety.

Here's the calculations on a 5% CD:

A $1,000 deposit earns a total of $157.63 in interest in three years.

A $5,000 deposit earns a total of $788.13 in interest in three years.

A $10,000 deposit earns a total of $1,576.25 in interest in three years.

Obviously, these figures must be adjusted depending on current CD interest rates. The advantage of CDs and other fixed income products is that no matter how poorly the stock market performs, your cash is safe, and the *principal* (i.e., the original amount deposited) doesn't change. Those who fear losing money may be attracted to CDs and other fixed income products.

In the real world, if you invest in the stock market, there is always a risk of losing money. It can't be avoided. If you invest in CDs or a money market account, however, your principal will always be waiting for you, plus interest.

Cash Is Not Trash

It's not how much money you make that determines whether you are wealthy, but how much you keep. That is why it's so vital to invest in the stock market while also keeping a healthy amount of cash on the side.

There is a name for people who have a lot of possessions, including big houses and cars, but little or no savings. They are called *cash poor*. All of these possessions don't help if you can't afford to pay for emergencies or to fix the house.

Therefore, make it a goal in life to do everything possible to save money while investing in the financial markets. It's possible to do both.

US Treasury Bonds

As mentioned several times, the reason that most investors buy fixed income is because they want safer investments. One of the most popular fixed income products is US Treasury bonds, which are backed by the full faith and credit of the US government.

By buying Treasury bonds, you are lending money to the US government for a given length of time, often 20 to 30 years (this is the *maturity date*). You can hold the bond for its entire lifetime or sell it before maturity. I want to repeat this: when buying Treasury bonds, you are lending money to the government.

In return, the government promises to pay back all the money plus interest. Each bond has a fixed interest rate that changes at auction every four months (when the Treasury issues new bonds). You have to pay federal income tax on the interest, but no state or local taxes.

You can buy Treasury bonds from your brokerage, bank, or directly from the US Treasury at treasurydirect.gov. The minimum investment is $100. Treasuries are issued in electronic form.

When buying a 30-year US Treasury bond with a 4% *coupon* rate (coupon is the interest rate), you'll receive $40 per year for each $1,000 invested. You are paid every six months until maturity.

Unlike other investments (the stock market, for example), US Treasury buyers know exactly how much interest they collect, and that the principal is safe. Treasury bonds are *liquid*, which means they can be bought and sold anytime.

In return for safety, and the promise that your principal will be returned with no loss, the interest rate received on the Treasury bond is on the low side. That is a fair trade-off accepted by every buyer of US Treasury notes, bills, and bonds.

However, if you want a higher return on your investments, you must take on additional risk. When investing in financial products with no such promise (i.e., guarantee), such as stocks, mutual funds, and ETFs, the potential return is greater. With no guarantees of making a profit, an investor accepts risk. In fact, the potential return may turn into a loss.

When buying Treasuries, however, unless the entire US government defaulted (i.e., missed an interest payment), you would continue to keep receiving those checks from the government as long as you hold the Treasury bond. Is the interest high enough to meet your financial needs? Only you can decide that.

Treasury Bills

T-bills are very short-term Treasuries with maturity dates that range from one month to one year. Because they are short term, the interest rate will likely be lower than with a Treasury bond. The minimum investment is $100.

Treasury Notes

Treasury notes have intermediate maturity dates of 2, 5, or 10 years. They also have a fixed interest rate and a $100 minimum investment.

DRIP (DIVIDEND REINVESTMENT PLAN)

A *dividend reinvestment plan* (DRIP) enables a shareholder to purchase shares of stock directly from a company. Any dividends received are automatically used to buy more shares (they are reinvested).

These plans have different names such as a DIP (direct investment plan), DSPs (direct stock plans), or DPPs (direct purchase plans). Before enrolling in any of these plans, be certain that you want to participate in the company's stock. Keep in mind that some companies charge fees, so find out the details before joining the plan.

Typically, DRIPs are no-fee or low-cost plans, whereas DSPs may charge high fees and even commissions. As with all DRIPs, there is a minimum investment to join the plan. To avoid surprises, do your homework, and that means asking some basic questions before signing up. There is no need to buy any plan that charges a commission.

Why would you want a DRIP? It enables you to buy stock directly from a corporation rather than through your broker. For many investors, it's more convenient to buy through a brokerage. Compare the costs involved before deciding.

Bottom line: Although DRIPs make sense for some investors, it is probably a better deal, and easier, to buy a DRIP through your broker and not directly from a corporation.

REAL ESTATE INVESTING

Hopefully by now you have a brokerage account with an S&P 500 index fund. Perhaps you added a few stocks. If you're looking for another way to generate wealth for you and your child, you may want to consider investing in real estate.

I'll give you a quick overview of real estate investing. If you want to learn more about this fascinating topic, I recommend buying real estate books or looking online at reputable sources, including newspapers and magazines. Real estate is always a hot topic so there is a lot of information.

One of the biggest misconceptions about real estate concerns your first house. Many people believe their house is an asset, but in reality, it's a liability. It's an asset when you own your second house and rent it to others. That's when your investment turns into a money-making machine (assuming all goes well).

If possible, you may want to include your child into any real estate transactions, or at least discuss what you are doing. To improve their financial literacy, take them through the house-buying process. With young children, one way to introduce them to real estate is by playing games such as Monopoly, but there are newer board games as well as virtual reality games.

Most schools don't teach real estate investing (or any investing for that matter), or even how to buy a house, although buying a house is one of the most important financial decisions most people make in their lifetimes.

If your child seems interested, you can give them a head start by showing them how it's done. You never know where that could lead.

Learning about real estate gives them an advantage over their peers, especially if they learn how to buy and sell properties.

Why Invest in Real Estate?

The number-one reason to invest in real estate, and be a potential landlord, is for cash flow. It's also wonderful when the asset (i.e., a house) you own rises in value (although there are no guarantees that it will).

According to research, real estate has appreciated by about 4% a year, but that varies depending on location. Obviously, real estate in some areas of the country has appreciated a lot more than in others. As real estate agents like to say, it's all about "location, location, location." Select the right location and your returns should easily exceed 4% per year.

There are a number of tax advantages that come with investing in real estate. The most popular is the ability to deduct business expenses, because in reality your real estate investment is a business. As always, see a tax professional for more specific tax-related advice.

Obstacles

Unfortunately, real estate doesn't always rise in value. Although not as volatile as stocks, there have been periods when real estate prices have plunged. That usually occurs as a result of weather-related damage such as from hurricanes, or environmental problems such as beach erosion or structural damage.

For all of these reasons, it is essential to do your homework before investing in any property. That means looking at the *comps* (i.e., the selling prices of comparable houses), doing a thorough inspection of the property, and negotiating for the best price.

Another negative is that real estate is *illiquid*; that is, it can sometimes be difficult to buy or sell a single, specific property. Unlike investing in index funds and stocks, you can't click on a button and purchase a house. It takes time to invest in properties. Also, not everyone has the time to do research before buying, finding tenants, and then managing the property.

Also, after becoming a landlord, unexpected problems may pop up. It could be a broken refrigerator or air conditioner, disrespectful tenants, or late payments. If you have the personality that can deal with these kind of problems and more, then real estate may be something to consider in the future.

One of the biggest obstacles is that most real estate investments require a large investment, not a few hundred dollars like with index funds but tens of thousands of dollars.

Finally, similar to investing in stocks, it's lots of fun when your house price moves higher (based on the latest selling price in the neighborhood), but not so enjoyable when selling prices have dropped. A more common problem occurs when a tenant doesn't pay rent on time, or disrespects (or even trashes) your property.

Your First Property

More than likely, the first property you buy will be a home that gives a roof over your head, and not a money-making investment. Some may contend that even your first home could generate income. For example, you could produce extra income by renting out a room in your house, which would turn your first home into an investment.

> Note: Some of you may be tempted to use the equity in your home as a money source using a HELOC (i.e., a home equity loan). Perhaps you want to make home improvements or use the money as a deposit for another house.

In my opinion, a HELOC is a terrible idea and should be avoided if at all possible. This risky product is really a credit card for your house. With a standard credit card, failure to make a payment results in a damaged credit rating. With a HELOC, failure to make a payment can result in foreclosure (i.e., losing your house). If possible, don't rely on a HELOC to bring in extra money.

Get Professional Help

In reality, buying property involves hiring professionals who can help you. Talking to your friends or acquaintances is not usually a great idea because most have fears and prejudices that may lead you in the wrong direction.

For example, one friend may be against all real estate investment because they once had a bad experience, or something they heard from someone else. Another friend might suggest that you do a "cash-out refinance" so you can borrow money to buy a new property. Instead of listening to well-meaning but uninformed friends, speak to a financial advisor who will give objective advice.

It's also a good idea to consult with a tax professional who can explain the benefits and disadvantages of buying an investment property. This person can give you tax strategies as well as let you know the tax benefits if you proceed with a purchase. A financial advisor with extensive real estate expertise may also be what you're looking for.

Lenders and Agents

It may take time to find a good lender that specializes in the kind of property you want to buy, and in a desirable location. Many people seek out a mortgage broker for help because they can help cut through the red tape to get a loan approved (assuming you need a loan).

It is also a good idea to find an experienced real estate agent who finds competitive deals on good properties. Real estate commissions are negotiable, and fortunately for buyers, they have dropped (thanks to a lawsuit settled in 2024 that reduces real estate agent commissions). A good agent will review the final contract (although it may be a good idea to hire a real estate attorney to review it as well).

Before buying, it's important to get an appraiser (the lender will insist on it) to determine the value of the property and if there are any deal-breaking defects. The appraiser not only protects the lender but also protects you from buying an undesirable or overvalued property.

Interest Rates

There are two basic types of interest rates: *fixed* or *variable* (and a few that combine both). Eventually, you will need to lock in a competitive interest rate when borrowing money. Locking in a competitive rate is one of the most important actions a homebuyer can make because it affects the monthly interest payment for the next 15 or 30 years.

For most people, a fixed rate mortgage is preferable because they always know the monthly mortgage payment. This gives many people peace of mind and a good night's sleep.

The downside to a fixed rate mortgage is that the fees are a little higher than a variable rate. However, with a variable interest rate, if you get caught on the wrong side of rising interest rates, you will rue the day you agreed to a rate that fluctuates over time. Variable rates can be extremely risky, so tread cautiously if agreeing to this method.

It's very important to discuss the various interest rate options with the people on your team, including your real estate broker, mortgage broker, or speak directly with the lender (if not using a mortgage broker).

Negotiating

After you find a decent property, negotiating for the best price can be challenging. Unfortunately, most people are poor negotiators. With help from a competent real estate agent, and doing your own research, you should have a pretty good idea of what is a reasonable price. Then it's up to you to try to get the seller to agree with your target price. I don't want to minimize the importance of this step: it's very important to evaluate what the house is worth, and what the seller is willing to accept.

A common problem is for buyers to pay well above the seller's asking price, especially in highly desirable areas. Try not to fall into that trap. If the house is in great demand by other potential buyers, there is little you can do to compete. It may be best to bide your time and not pay beyond your perception of the home's value.

Another problem is that some sellers are unreasonable. To succeed with any negotiation, it's important to be unemotional (just as you are when buying or selling stocks). If the seller will not agree to your price, you may have to walk away from the deal, or at least pretend to walk away. You can also cough up more money, which is like paying the market price for a stock when you should be entering a limit price. A good agent will help with your decision.

Your New Investment Property

Once a seller accepts your offer, congratulations! After you signed a number of documents, you have started your journey as a real estate investor. Hopefully, you will find wonderful tenants who will provide consistent cash flow for many years.

As mentioned, it's wise to include your child in some of these discussions. One day, they will have to buy their own house, and perhaps an investment property.

If you decide to buy real estate as an investment, keep in mind that the information in this chapter is only a broad overview. There are many twists and turns in the process, and a good real estate agent, mortgage broker, or lawyer, should guide you. There are also a number of books on buying real estate, which I urge you to buy if you are serious about investing in real estate.

Shorting Stocks

I'm going to introduce a risky strategy that you probably will never use, although it's a good idea to know it exists. It's called *shorting* (or *short-selling*). When shorting stocks, you are betting that the stock price, or the entire market, will go down. The farther the stock or market falls, the more money the investor makes.

The reason it's so risky is this: potential losses are unlimited. Let me explain. When going long (i.e., bullish), the most you can lose on a stock is all the cash you invested. Yes, that's bad. When shorting, however, investors can theoretically lose an infinite sum of money. How high can a stock price go? There is no limit.

Imagine if you had been shorting stocks like Amazon, Yahoo, Walmart, Microsoft, or thousands of other companies. For every point that the stock price rallied, you would lose money. The shorting strategy is for traders who plan to exit the trade quickly (and can also meet strict margin requirements). That is why shorting is not recommended for most people (including any older children who might be tempted to try this strategy).

I know of professional short sellers who got caught in a *meltup*—when the market rapidly moved higher for no clear reason except that machine-driven computer algos (i.e., algorithms) pushed stock prices "to the moon," crushing any short sellers caught on the wrong side of the trade.

How Shorting Is Done

For those who are still interested, here is how it's done. First, on your brokerage screen, press the button that says, "Short." Some brokerages may ask you to press the "Sell" button first. In fact, shorting means you are selling shares of a stock that you don't even own.

Eventually, you must buy back those shares. If you can purchase those shares at a lower price, you will have made money. If you buy those shares at a higher price, you will have lost money. Truthfully, many people find it confusing to sell something they don't own.

The Risks

In addition to the unlimited amount of money you can lose if on the wrong side of the trade, there are other risks. Traders must use a margin account to sell anything short. That means you must borrow money from the broker to use this strategy.

I don't expect most people reading this book to short stocks, but during a bear market, some might be tempted to try this strategy. If so, I suggest you first see the movie, *The Big Short*, which explores the psychological grief that many short sellers experience, even when they are right.

In the movie, a group of short sellers correctly predict that the housing market would collapse. But because they shorted too early, it caused them enormous paper losses and pain. Eventually they were proved right and made millions of dollars on the trades, but emotionally it was very costly.

How GameStop Helped Destroy Short Sellers

Another fascinating short-selling story involved GameStop (GME), a struggling brick-and-mortar retailer. Many on Wall Street thought the stock was doomed to fail, so they accumulated millions of dollars in short positions.

Unbeknownst to the Wall Street pros (hedge funds), thousands of bullish retail investors gathered on Reddit, a popular internet forum. The leader of the group was "Roaring Kitty," a 34-year-old Massachusetts dad who ran a YouTube channel from his basement.

Urged on by Roaring Kitty, the traders on Reddit collectively bought millions of shares of GameStop, causing the stock to surge over 1,500% within weeks, sending volatility and the stock price to the moon. The stock went from $3 per share to $483 in less than two months for no valid reason.

Melvin Capital, an investment fund that heavily shorted GameStop, reportedly lost hundreds of millions of dollars on the trade. It was also reported that some hedge funds, along with thousands of retail short sellers, collectively lost $6 billion shorting this one stock. This true story demonstrates how risky it is to short stocks. If short-selling pros can lose their shirts, then retail investors don't have a chance.

An entertaining comedy drama, *Dumb Money* (2023), describes what happened to the GameStop traders, including how Roaring Kitty became an instant multimillionaire when he finally sold his GameStop shares near the top.

Bottom line: Although shorting may be an intriguing strategy, most investors should focus on buying and holding index funds or stocks. It's usually a mistake to bet against the Wall Street machine.

CONCLUSION

Guess what? You just finished the last chapter of the book! After a few closing comments, all that is left is a list of down-to-earth definitions, useful websites and apps, further research, and the index. Thanks for taking the time to read my entire book. I appreciate it!

CLOSING
COMMENTS

Congratulations for finishing my book! I admire that you took the time to read it all. It's not that easy to learn about the stock market, so I applaud you for doing so. It was an honor to share with you some of the lessons and strategies that I learned so you can pass them on to your children.

I hope that my book was an interesting read and that it offered ideas about how to build wealth for you and your child. It would be wonderful if you could use the stock market to improve your lives.

Hopefully, this book will help your children understand how the market works. Unfortunately, stocks, bonds, index funds, the economy, personal finance, and investing are not high priorities for most schools (except to play "The Stock Market Game" in high school). Therefore, it is up to you to fill in the gaps.

One of my goals in writing this book is to give your child the confidence and courage to manage and invest on their own. If they can successfully adopt these skills, they may grow up being financially independent with the freedom to do whatever they want in life.

With any luck, your children may switch from being only spenders to also becoming investors. If they can think like investors, they will look at companies not only as a consumer does but also how to become a stockholder.

Think about this: instead of spending all their money to buy the newest Apple iPhone, if they would have used a portion of that cash to invest in Apple stock, they could have made enough money to buy a dozen iPhones.

Before I let you go, here are a few more thoughts.

AVOID CREDIT CARD DEBT

The way that most people get hurt financially is by spending too much money using credit cards, and then getting trapped in a compound interest nightmare. The goal is to get rid of bad credit card debt (and sickeningly high interest rates) while setting aside money for investments. It's possible to do both.

Most important, teach your children the danger of spending money on things they can't afford. If anything, they should be taught that credit card debt must be avoided at all costs, even if they must wait for things they want to buy.

It makes no sense to pay more than 20% in credit card interest while aiming to make 10% with investments. Credit card debt must be treated as a skunk at a party, or better yet, as an albatross that will prevent them from reaching their financial goals.

If they don't control debt, then debt will take over every aspect of their lives. Yes, they may have to wait for the things they want, but it's better than paying outrageous credit card fees and interest. Credit card debt will do lasting damage to their finances.

Do you want your children to be smart spenders or knowledgeable investors? In reality, they can do both. Before your child gets their first credit card, teach them how to make money work for them by investing in the stock market with index funds and to avoid all credit card debt.

One solution is to have them use a debit card rather than a credit card. With a debit card, they can see the money in the account dropping as they spend money. They will quickly learn that "money doesn't grow on trees."

MINIMIZE RISK

To succeed in the financial markets, it's crucial to minimize risk. Although it's impossible to eliminate all financial risks, there are ways to reduce it. For example, put some money in safe places such as CDs or a money market account. This account can be used for emergencies.

Another way to lower risk is to monitor investments each month or quarter. It's important to track profits and losses. Teach your children to take control of their finances early in life.

HOW TO BUILD WEALTH

I hope you find ways to help your child produce wealth. Discuss the idea of investing in index funds with a goal of being a millionaire before retirement (which may seem like 1,000 years away to some teenagers). Investing in an index fund may not be exciting, but watching money grow over a long time period is a pleasant experience.

There are a number of bestselling books that suggest all you need to do to get rich is to hope and wish for it to happen. Although I'm a big believer in positive thinking, becoming wealthy requires more than wishing or hoping. You must prepare, plan, and act, and that means opening a brokerage account and investing (even if it's only $10 per month).

There is no time to make excuses or procrastinate. Yes, there may be some tough moments ahead because the stock market behaves more like a rollercoaster than a rocket ship. When the market is moving lower, grit your teeth and follow the dollar cost averaging strategy laid out in this book.

As you already know, one of the biggest threats to the success of your child's investing strategy is withdrawing money. As their investment account grows larger, it becomes hard for most people to resist the temptation to sell some or all of their investments for an emergency (a vacation to Spain is not an emergency!). If you're lucky, they won't sell (unless they have a 529 college savings plan, which they will use for educational expenses and tuition). No one said it was easy.

If they do withdraw the money, they will lose dividends, compound earnings growth, and a rising stock market. As you already know, the secret sauce for building wealth is adding to an index fund each month and letting it grow.

Investing is all about making money, but it is more than that. An even better investment is in people. You can't go wrong spending money on your child and other close family members, a new business, your child's education, pets, or those who desperately need your help. After all, why make money if you don't use it to improve your life and the lives of the people you know?

GOOD LUCK

Good luck with your investments. It's been a pleasure sharing my knowledge and experiences. I hope that you and your children's financial dreams come true, and that a huge pot of money is waiting for them as they grow older.

Thanks again for reading my book. If you have comments or questions, feel free to send an email to msincere@gmail.com. Also, if you notice any errors, please let me know and I will make corrections in the next edition. Finally, if you have time, feel free to visit my website, www.michaelsincere.com.

GLOSSARY: UNDERSTANDABLE DEFINITIONS

INTRODUCTION

In this glossary, I did something different. As a former teacher, my job was to simplify complex ideas and vocabulary words so that my students could understand them. In this glossary, I decided to use those same skills to make financial definitions understandable to you and your children.

If you are new to the stock market, you may find these definitions helpful, so in each definition, I included a sentence that includes the vocabulary word. This should help you and your child better understand the meaning of the word.

If you want more detailed definitions of any of the following vocabulary words, go to the website, Investopedia (https://www.investopedia.com/). You will get a full explanation of each word.

And now, for your reading pleasure, here are important financial definitions with a sample sentence.

401(k) and 403(b) plans Special investment plans offered to their employees by some companies as a tool for saving money for retirement. Some people don't sign up for the plans because they might not understand they are receiving free money. Another benefit: taxes are not paid on the money until the money is distributed (not earlier than age 59½). **Sentence:** It is a great idea to enroll in a company's *401(k) plan*.

529 plan An investment plan for children that allows tax-free withdrawals as long as they are used for qualified educational expenses such as tuition, books, and other school-related expenses. The two 529 plans are the educational savings plans and prepaid tuition plans. **Sentence:** Many parents like the *529 plan* because it helps pay for their children's education.

Algorithm A sophisticated computer program designed to automatically perform simple to complex tasks using step-by-step instructions. From automatically buying and selling stocks to writing a thesis, algorithms are useful tools for humans, and becoming more popular each year. **Sentence:** Many *algorithms* are replacing jobs that humans once performed.

Annual report A lengthy and typically unexciting document that reveals important information about a company. This report can be found online. Some of the stuff in the annual report is useful, such as the balance sheet and income statement, but it's mostly public relations material, bragging how great it is. **Sentence:** Some of the most interesting and revealing information in an *annual report* is hidden in the fine print.

Ask price A market quote consists of two prices: the bid price and the ask price. The ask price is always higher than the bid price and is the lowest "published" price that a seller will accept for a stock or other security. **Sentence:** When buying a stock, buy at or near the *ask price*.

Asset   Something of value that is owned such as a car, phone, or house. Assets include investments such as stocks, bonds, mutual funds, or index funds. **Sentence:** Some people have a lot of financial *assets* including stocks, bonds, and real estate.

Asset allocation   An investing method that divides or splits up the things that investors own (i.e., assets). For example, an investor using asset allocation may have a portfolio that includes stocks, bonds, and cash. **Sentence:** *Asset allocation* is one way of reducing risk when investing in the stock market.

Balance sheet   A report card for a company that describes how much money they earn and how much they spend. **Sentence:** To find out more about a company, it's a good idea to look at its *balance sheet*.

Bear (or bearish)   The name for investors or traders who believe that the value of assets (usually stocks or the entire stock market) will fall, and keep falling. **Sentence:** Many investors are *bearish* about the stock market right now.

Bear market   When the stock market has fallen by at least 20% from its previous high, it is considered to be in a bear market. Investors do not like bear markets because they are usually losing money. **Sentence:** Oh no! It must be a *bear market* because the stock market keeps moving lower and lower.

Bid price   When buying a stock, two prices are always shown: the bid price and the ask price. The bid price is always lower than the ask price and is the highest "published" price that any buyer will pay for that asset at that precise moment in time. **Sentence:** When selling stocks, sell at or near the *bid price*.

Blue-chip stocks   The name for stocks that are considered to be the best in their field with an excellent reputation and a large market capitalization.

Blue-chips are the most valuable chips in poker. **Sentence:** Many investors buy only *blue-chip*, dividend-paying stocks because they are the finest stocks in the world.

Bond   A loan from an investor to a company or government in exchange for regular interest payments for a set time period. **Sentence:** Instead of buying an individual *bond*, many investors buy a bond ETF.

Brokerage account   After signing up with a brokerage firm, investors are given a brokerage account, where they can buy and sell stocks, bonds, or other assets. **Sentence:** Investors open a *brokerage account* online or in person through a brokerage firm.

Brokerage firm   A company that arranges transactions between buyers and sellers of assets, including stocks, bonds, mutual funds, and ETFs. **Sentence:** Investors buy and sell stocks and other financial products from a *brokerage firm*.

Brokerage statement   A summary of all transactions made in the investment account over the prior month. It also lists the current value of each asset in the account, including uninvested cash. **Sentence:** Each month, investors receive their *brokerage statement*, which lists what they own and all transactions from the previous month.

Bubble   A phenomenon when the stock market (or other asset) has risen so high that it could pop like a balloon at any time. A bubble is dangerous for investors because a "pop" is a rapid and intense decline in the asset's price, and often occurs with little or no warning. **Sentence:** There is nothing more unpredictable and dangerous than a market *bubble*, when stocks seemed to be going to the moon (i.e., rising with no end in sight).

Bull (or bullish)   A person who believes an asset's price will move higher. Bulls want the market to move higher, and bears want the market to move lower. **Sentence:** Investors are *bullish* about the stock market.

Bull market   When the stock market has been moving higher for a long time period, and is 20% above the previous low point. Investors are happy about a bull market because they make money when the market price of the investments they own increases. **Sentence:** Yeah! We are in a *bull market* because stocks keep going higher every month.

Capital gain A stock or other asset that has increased in value and is selling for a profit. **Sentence:** Investors who sell their stocks for a profit have a *capital gain* and must pay taxes on the profits.

Capital loss A stock or other asset that has decreased in value and is selling at a loss. **Sentence:** Investors who sell any asset at a loss must report that *capital loss* on their income tax form.

Certificate of deposit (CD) A financial product that enables investors to earn interest from a bank (or other financial company). Typically, the CD term ranges from a few months to five years. **Sentence:** According to the rules, investors who buy a *certificate of deposit* cannot cancel those CDs prior to maturity without paying a penalty.

Commission A service fee charged by a broker for completing a financial transaction. At one time, there was a commission charge for making any stock transaction, but not anymore. Nevertheless, some brokers still charge fees for their work. **Sentence:** Brokers used to charge a *commission* for buying or selling stocks, but most brokers do not.

Commodities Raw materials or agricultural products that are bought and sold on an exchange. Examples include gold, oil, gas, coffee, and wheat. Professional traders buy and sell commodity contracts, but they sell those contracts before the maturity date so that do not take delivery of the commodity. **Sentence:** It's not easy to trade *commodities* so only those with a lot of experience should buy or sell them.

Compounding A way of earning more money from an investment. Compound interest is the interest earned on interest that was already made when that interest was reinvested. **Sentence:** In real life, *compounding* is how investors can build wealth with any investment, and also how credit card companies get rich.

Contract   A written or verbal agreement that is backed by law. **Sentence:** Do not sign a *contract* with another person unless a lawyer or other professional first looks at it.

Correction   When the stock market (or any asset) falls by more than 10% from its recent high. **Sentence:** The stock market is currently in a *correction*.

Crash   When the stock market (or asset) suddenly drops in price by such a large amount that investors are afraid. Typically, it's the number-one news story on the internet or TV. For example, if the stock market fell by more than 20% over one or two days, that would be a crash. The biggest crashes in history were in 1929 and 1987. **Sentence:** The stock market looks like it's going to *crash*! It has been dropping by large amounts every day this week.

Cryptocurrency   An electronic or digital currency created by computer code. The most well-known cryptocurrency is Bitcoin, which has been on a rollercoaster ride ever since it was first invented in 2009. **Sentence:** *Cryptocurrencies* are very popular, but also very volatile because most people don't know their true value.

Custodial account   A savings or investment account set up by an adult for a child under 18 years old (or 21 in some states). **Sentence:** Setting up a *custodial account* makes sense for many parents as long as they understand that the minor takes control of the account when reaching adulthood (18 or 21 years old).

Discipline   A characteristic or trait of an investor who follows an investment strategy and a set of rules while also remaining unemotional when making or losing money. **Sentence:** Investors who are *disciplined* have a much better chance to make money in the stock market.

Discount broker   (see *Online broker*).

Dividend   Money received from owning shares of stock in a company. Some investors buy only stocks that pay dividends. Many people live off the dividends while other investors reinvest them. Investors who own

182

dividend stocks receive a check from the corporation or reinvest the dividend to buy additional shares. **Sentence:** Companies share their profits with shareholders in the form of *dividends.*

Dividend Reinvestment Plan (DRIP) A program set up by a brokerage firm or corporation that enables investors to buy additional shares of stock by automatically reinvesting cash dividends. **Sentence:** Investors may enroll in a *DRIP* with their brokerage firm or directly with the corporation that issues the stock as a way to compound their earnings.

Dividend stocks Stocks in strong, well-known companies that have a history of paying dividends to investors who own their stock. Dividend stocks are also called *income stocks.* **Sentence:** Many investors prefer to buy *dividend stocks* as an income source.

Diversification/diversified A risk-reducing strategy for investors that mixes several types of investments. The goal is to reduce the risk of a specific stock or industry, causing a significant loss in an investor's portfolio. For example, investors may have an account with stocks, bonds, and cash. **Sentence:** Index funds, ETFs, and mutual funds are *diversified* because they include many stocks from different industries and sectors.

Dow Jones Industrial Average (DJIA or the Dow) A popular stock market index that follows 30 well-known industrial stocks that are considered to be some of the best in the world (i.e., blue-chip stocks). When people talk about the "market," they are usually talking about the Dow Jones Industrial Average. **Sentence:** How did the *Dow* do today?

Earnings The term used to describe a company's profit or loss. Typically, an earnings report is published quarterly. **Sentence:** The company's *earnings* were excellent last year so the stock price moved higher.

Earnings per share (EPS) One of the ways that investors use to measure how much investors are paying for each dollar of earnings. The EPS, displayed on many financial websites, gives an investor a good picture of whether a company's stock is over- or underpriced. **Sentence:** Many investors won't buy stock in a company if the *EPS* is negative.

Emergency fund   A sum of cash stored in a bank savings account, CD, or money market account that is available in case of emergency. **Sentence:** Careful people have an *emergency fund* in case they need money quickly without relying on a credit card.

Exchange-traded fund (ETF)   A basket of stocks or other securities in a specific sector or asset class. There are thousands of ETFs consisting of every conceivable type of financial product from stocks, bonds, real estate, and fixed income to commodities and cryptocurrencies. **Sentence:** Many investors and traders buy *ETFs* because fees are low and they can be bought and sold easily during the day.

FOMO (fear of missing out)   When a trader is afraid that if they don't act now, they will miss out on a big, money-making opportunity. Usually, they lose money on the panic-driven trade. **Sentence:** I'm so afraid that I'm going to miss out on this trade (*FOMO*) that I'm going to buy the stock right now, regardless of the price.

Federal Reserve System (the Fed)   Created in 1913, the Federal Reserve oversees all of the banks and helps to manage the economy by raising or lowering interest rates as needed, among other tasks. The seven members of the Board of Governors are in control of the Fed, with the chairman holding tremendous powers. **Sentence:** The *Fed* is meeting Tuesday and Wednesday this month to discuss the possibility of lowering interest rates.

Financial advisor   A person who gets paid to guide investors in managing their personal finances and investments. **Sentence:** I am thinking of talking with a *financial advisor* to be sure I am on the right financial path.

Fundamental analysis   A method used to determine a stock's fair market value by analyzing the company's financials. That includes how much it earns and spends, and whether the managers are doing a good job. **Sentence:** I plan to use *fundamental analysis* before I buy my next stock.

Good 'til canceled (GTC)   A type of order telling the brokerage to keep the order live until it is filled or the investor cancels it. **Sentence:** I always place a *GTC* order on any stock that I want to buy so that I do not miss buying the stock when it declines to my limit price.

Growth stocks   Stocks in companies that are expected to increase earnings every year without interruption. Often, growth stocks are expensive because investors are willing to pay more for the chance to make good money. **Sentence:** I plan to diversify by buying shares of *growth stocks* in addition to buying dividend-paying stocks.

Hedge   A strategy used by investors and traders to reduce risk. For investors, hedging includes diversifying investments. Traders, however, may use complex methods to hedge, including using call and put options to protect stock positions against a large loss. **Sentence:** I am going to *hedge* my stock position by owning some bonds.

Income stocks   (see *Dividend stocks*).

Index/indexes   A group or basket of stocks or other financial products. Index examples: S&P 500, Dow Jones Industrial Average, and the Nasdaq 100. **Sentence:** I really like trading *indexes* such as SPY and QQQ, which are index ETFs.

Inflation   An economic phenomenon that occurs when the price of goods or services rises over time. **Sentence:** The prices at the supermarket and other stores are rising because of *inflation*.

Interest   The amount paid by borrowers of money to the lenders. **Sentence:** *Interest* is wonderful to receive but not so fun to pay.

Interest rate   The amount earned from fixed income such as a CD, savings account, bond, or money market account (expressed as a percentage). It is also the amount that lenders charge to those who borrow money. **Sentence:** Before taking out a mortgage on a house, it's very important to know the current *interest rate.*

Investment strategy A plan that helps investors make investment decisions. The strategy is created based on investors' goals, how much risk they are willing to take (i.e., risk tolerance), and how soon they need the money. **Sentence:** An *investment strategy* for long-term investors, who are willing to patiently wait, differs from that of short-term traders, who want a faster payoff.

Investor Someone who attempts to make a profit with the least amount of risk and the highest return over a long time period. **Sentence:** *Investors* buy stocks hoping to make a profit.

IRA (Individual Retirement Account) A tax-deferred account set up at a financial institution with the objective of saving for retirement. Early withdrawals before the age of 59½ are taxed and penalized. **Sentence:** I can open a tax-free Roth IRA using after-tax income or a regular *IRA* where tax payments are deferred until withdrawal.

Joint brokerage account An account shared by two people such as a parent and child, or husband and wife. **Sentence:** There are three types of *joint brokerage accounts*, so speak to your broker to find which one meets your needs.

Large-cap stocks Cap refers to a stock's capitalization, or the total value of all its outstanding shares. Any stock that has a *market capitalization* (see *Market capitalization*) of between $10 billion and $200 billion is a large-cap stock. In other words, these are really big companies! **Sentence:** Apple, Microsoft, Amazon, Meta, Tesla, and Nvidia are all popular *large-cap* stocks.

Leverage Using borrowed money (i.e., going into debt) to increase the size of an investment with the intention of earning additional profits. This is a double-edged sword because it can also result in the loss of additional money. Buying a home with a mortgage, investing in a business, or borrowing money to buy stocks are examples of using leverage. **Sentence:** Many people use *leverage* to buy a house because they don't have enough money to buy it with cash.

Limit order   An order to buy or sell any asset that specifies the maximum price to pay, or the minimum offer to accept when buying or selling. For example, an investor can place a limit order with their broker to buy XYZ at $33 per share. They will pay $33 or possibly less per share, but never more than that. **Sentence:** It's a good idea to buy stocks with a *limit order* rather than a market order.

Liquidity   Refers to how quickly and easily stocks can be bought or sold. When volume in the stock market is high, liquidity is high. **Sentence:** It's usually a good idea to buy stocks that are *liquid*, or have a lot of *liquidity*.

Load mutual fund   A mutual fund that charges sales commissions, or sales fees. These fees can range from 5% to as high as 10% for some specialized funds. **Sentence:** If possible, avoid buying a *load mutual fund* and instead choose a no-load mutual fund.

Long-term investment   Any investment held for a long time period, typically at least one year. **Sentence:** Many people buy shares of an index fund as a *long-term investment*.

Margin   Going on margin means an investor or trader borrows money from the brokerage to buy additional shares of stock or other financial product. **Sentence:** It is usually not a good idea to buy stocks on *margin* because of the increased risks.

Margin call   When the value of an investor's portfolio declines, the brokerage firm requires the customer to send more money to meet the "minimum capital requirements." This is another way of saying they owe too much money to the brokerage relative to the value of the portfolio. If that additional cash is not available, the broker will sell some of the assets to minimize their own risk. **Sentence:** It's always bad news to receive a *margin call* from the broker, who says that money is needed to meet the margin requirements.

Market capitalization   The total number of shares multiplied by the current share price equals the market capitalization. There are small-cap, mid-cap, and large-cap stocks depending on the number. Example: A company selling at $50 per share with 20 million shares has a market cap of $1 billion, and is considered to be a small-cap stock. **Sentence:** Many people look at the *market capitalization* before investing their money in a stock.

Market order   An order to buy or sell shares of stock at the current market price without negotiating for a better price. The worst time to place a market order is during a fast-moving market, when such an order is risky. In this example, although the order may be filled, it will likely be at a poor price. **Sentence:** I placed a *market order* with my online broker to sell my stock at the best available price right now.

Mental stop price   Instead of entering a hard or real "stop price" to sell any shares owned, investors think of a price in their head. When that mental or imaginary price is reached, disciplined investors enter the real order. **Sentence:** I set a *mental stop price* at $15 per share, when I will sell the stock.

Mid-cap stocks   Companies with a market capitalization between $2 billion and $10 billion. **Sentence:** *Mid-cap stocks* have the potential to grow faster than large-cap stocks and less quickly than small-cap stocks.

Mutual fund   An investment that "pools" money from many investors. Professional fund managers use that pooled money to invest in a diversified assortment of stocks, bonds, fixed income and other financial products. **Sentence:** Many people like to buy *mutual funds* because professional money managers control the account and buy and sell stocks for the fund's shareholders.

Nasdaq-100   A capitalization-weighted index that includes 100 of the largest and most actively traded companies listed on the Nasdaq stock exchange. **Sentence:** People who want to invest or trade in technology stocks often choose the Invesco exchange-traded fund, QQQ, which tracks the *Nasdaq-100* index.

Nasdaq Composite Index (Nasdaq)   A stock market index containing more than 2,500 stocks, many that are in the technology sector. **Sentence:** The *Nasdaq Composite Index* is a very popular index strongly weighted with technology stocks.

New York Stock Exchange (NYSE)   Located in New York, the NYSE is the largest stock exchange in the world. It is a marketplace for stocks, where buyers and sellers meet to buy and sell any stock that is listed on the exchange. Most trading is now done online rather than in person. **Sentence:** In the old days, traders used to meet in person at the *NYSE* to trade stocks and every other type of security.

Online broker   A brokerage firm that fills customer orders at a low cost but does not offer any investment advice. Because so many people want to do their own trading, online brokers have exploded in popularity, driving commissions and fees lower. **Sentence:** An *online broker* is very different from a full-service broker, who charges high fees for their services.

Options   A sophisticated financial product that enables buyers and sellers to hedge, speculate, and protect an underlying asset such as a stock. Option strategies range from simple (e.g., selling covered calls) to complex (e.g., spreads). **Sentence:** One of the *option* strategies risk-adverse investors like to use is selling covered calls.

Overbought   A stock or market selling for much more than its true worth. Overbought stocks can keep moving higher (and become more overbought) before the price moves so high that it reverses direction. **Sentence:** It's not a good idea to buy stocks that are *overbought* because they could reverse direction at any time.

Oversold   A stock or market selling for much less than its true worth. Stocks that are oversold can keep moving lower (and become more oversold) before the price moves so low that it reverses direction. **Sentence:** If the timing is right, buying an *oversold* stock can be profitable.

Paper trading (simulated trading)   Many brokerage firms and some financial institutions allow investors and traders to buy and sell pretend shares with "play" money that simulates investing money in the stock market. **Sentence:** Many wise beginners *paper trade* before investing real money into the stock market.

P/E ratio (price/earnings ratio)   A fundamental indicator that compares a stock price to its earnings, displaying a ratio. In general, the lower the number, the better. However, some growth stocks may be a great investment even with a high P/E, whereas a low P/E stock doesn't always mean it is a good buy. **Sentence:** Many investors want to know the *P/E ratio* before making an investment.

Penny stocks   Junky stocks priced below $3 per share. These stocks are for those who want to speculate, not invest. Unfortunately, very few people make money buying penny stocks, which is why most investors should avoid trading them. **Sentence:** *Penny stocks* appear to be a great opportunity to make money because there is so little to lose, but losing money is the likely outcome.

Portfolio   A collection of investments such as stocks, bonds, index funds, ETFs, mutual funds, and cash. **Sentence:** When you create an investment *portfolio*, think of how much risk you are willing to take (i.e., what is your risk tolerance) and whether the portfolio is diversified.

Principal   The original sum of money invested. **Sentence:** When bonds mature, investors are pleased to receive a return of their *principal* plus interest.

Pump-and-dump   A scam that involves using social media and other methods to spread lies about a stock, encouraging unwitting investors to buy the stock and drive the price higher. As the price rallies, the scammers dump their shares, causing the stock to crash. That leaves investors holding the bag with huge losses. **Sentence:** A *pump-and-dump* scheme is a popular way of separating investors from their money.

Redemption fee   A fee charged to mutual fund investors when shares are sold within a certain time period, usually 30 days. **Sentence:** To discourage investors from selling shares soon after buying them (typically less than 30 days), a mutual fund company may charge a *redemption fee.*

Risk tolerance   Describes how much risk investors are willing to take when owning an asset. Those with high risk tolerance tend to take more chances, and buy more volatile stocks. Those with low risk tolerance tend to buy low-volatile or dividend stocks along with fixed income products. **Sentence:** Sadly, too many investors learn their degree of *risk tolerance* after they've lost money.

Robo-advisor   An automated, low-cost financial advisor with little or no human interaction that uses algorithms to create a balanced, diversified portfolio for investors. Some hybrid robo-advisors have both automated managers as well as human advisors. **Sentence:** In recent years, *robo-advisors* have gained in popularity.

Roth IRA (Individual Retirement Account)   A plan that enables investors to invest after-tax income into a variety of investments including stocks, ETFs, mutual funds, and index funds. Investors can withdraw the money from the account tax-free after age 59½. Investors should consult with a financial advisor or accountant because the rules periodically change over time. **Sentence:** A *Roth IRA* is an excellent tax-free vehicle for building wealth.

Savings account   A low-interest-rate cash account in a bank that is typically used for emergencies or for short-term savings goals. **Sentence:** Most children start their financial journey with a *savings account.*

SEC (Securities and Exchange Commission)   An independent federal agency with five members whose mission is to protect investors by preventing fraud, disclose important market information, and promote fair "dealing." The SEC monitors transactions and flags any trades that seem suspicious. Because SEC members are appointed by the president, enforcement of the rules varies depending on the party of the current administration. **Sentence:** The *SEC* was formed to help police the financial markets.

Security Anything of value that can be bought and sold on a public exchange, such as stocks and bonds. **Sentence:** People buy stocks and other *securities* when investing.

Shares Units of stock that indicate ownership, typically in a corporation. Those who own shares are called *shareholders* in the corporation. It gives them voting rights and enables investors to "share" in the success or failure of the company. **Sentence:** I bought 100 *shares* of stock in a technology company.

Shorting (short-selling) A sophisticated strategy used by bearish traders who profit when the price of a stock or index declines. The lower the price moves, the larger the trader's profit. **Sentence:** *Shorting* is a risky strategy, especially during a bull market.

Simulated trading (see *Paper trading*).

Small-cap stocks Stocks in a company whose market capitalization is more than $300 million but less than $2 billion. **Sentence:** Investors with higher-than-average risk tolerance like to buy *small-cap stocks*.

Socially responsible investing (SRI) A strategy used by investors or fund managers to seek out companies that invest in socially acceptable products. This means not investing in tobacco, gambling, alcohol, polluters, or anything that may be harmful to people or the environment. Nevertheless, investors want to make a profit while investing in "socially conscious" businesses. **Sentence:** *Socially responsible investing* has become more popular in recent years.

S&P 500 (Standard & Poor's 500) An index of the 500 largest US companies when measured by market capitalization. It is the benchmark that most fund managers want to beat, and the index that buy-and-hold investors want to match. **Sentence:** The *S&P 500* is one of the most important indexes in the world.

Stock   A term that represents partial ownership of a corporation. Investors and traders buy and sell shares of stock. **Sentence:** As *stock* prices rise or fall, investors make or lose money.

Stock chart   A graph or chart that displays the price history of a stock, or any investment, over a certain time period. By looking at a stock chart, investors and traders can get clues as to future price direction. Stock charts show a lot of information, including the most recent price, highs and lows, volume, and whether a stock is overbought or oversold. **Sentence:** *Stock charts* are displayed in different formats such as candlestick, line, or bar.

Stock exchange   A marketplace where buyers and sellers meet virtually to buy and sell stocks, bonds, and other financial products. The New York Stock Exchange (NYSE) is the largest in the world. **Sentence:** It used to be exciting to visit a *stock exchange* and watch traders wave their arms while buying and selling stocks. Now, almost all stock and bond trading is done online.

Stock market   A collection of all of the stock exchanges. The stock market refers to the entire financial market whereas a stock exchange refers to one location (such as the NYSE). **Sentence:** Investing in the *stock market* is one of the best ways to build wealth.

Stock sectors   A group of stocks that are in similar industries. The 11 stock sectors are health care, materials, real estate, consumer staples, consumer discretionary, financials, energy, industrials, consumer services, utilities, and technology. **Sentence:** There are many *stock sectors* for investors to choose from, but technology is always a favorite.

Stock split   An accounting maneuver done by the board of directors to increase the number of shares outstanding. Typically, stock split ratios are 2 for 1 or 3 for 1. Although it appears to be a bonanza for shareholders, the market capitalization remains the same as before the split. For example, if a $60 stock splits 3 for 1, each stockholder now owns three times as many shares, but the stock price will be $20 per share. Nevertheless, stock splits tend to be bullish because many investors feel that the lower stock price after the split makes it more attractive to own. That often results in a rising stock price. **Sentence:** Many investors are interested in buying a stock after a company announces a *stock split*.

> Note: The opposite of a stock split is a *reverse stock split*, an accounting maneuver that causes the share price to be artificially boosted to attract investor interest. A reverse stock split is a warning sign the company may be in trouble.

Stock quote (or quotation)   The market price of a stock that includes the current bid and ask price, along with the price of the most recent trade. **Sentence:** Investors always want to know the most recent *stock quote*.

Stop order (market or limit)   A stop order notifies the stock exchange through a broker to automatically convert the stop order into a market or limit order if and when the stock trades at (or through) the stop price. The stop (sell) order is not perfect, but it does reduce risk by limiting losses. Selling the shares when the price falls to a predetermined level is a good method for unloading a poor-performing stock. **Sentence:** An investor placed a *stop market order* to sell shares if the stock trades at, or lower than, $15 per share because they didn't want to lose money below that price.

Strategy   (see *Investment strategy*).

Symbol (ticker symbol)   A combination of letters or numbers that identify a specific stock or other financial product on an exchange. For example, the ticker symbol for Amazon is AMZN. The ticker symbol for Nvidia is NVDA. The symbol for the S&P 500 index is SPX.

Sentence: After investing or trading for a few weeks, it's easy to remember the *ticker symbol* for favorite stocks.

Technical analysis   A method of analyzing the market using stock charts and indicators to gain clues as to which direction the market is likely to move over the short term (from minutes to weeks or longer). **Sentence:** Before buying or selling a stock, many traders use *technical analysis* to confirm whether that is a wise move.

Ticker symbol   (see *Symbol*).

Trader   An individual who buys and sells stocks and other financial products seeking short-term gains. **Sentence:** It's not easy being a *trader* but many people use trading strategies every day.

Treasury bills   A US government debt security with a 1- to 12-month maturity date. **Sentence:** Investors seeking a safe short-term investment but with lower returns buy *Treasury bills*.

Treasury bonds   A US government debt security with a maturity date of 10 to 30 years. **Sentence:** Investors seeking a safe long-term investment are willing to accept lower returns and purchase *Treasury bonds*.

Treasury notes   A US government debt security with a maturity date of 1 to 10 years. **Sentence:** Investors seeking a safe medium-term investment but with lower returns buy *Treasury notes*.

UGMA (Uniform Transfers to Minors Act)   Allows an adult to transfer money into a custodial brokerage account on behalf of a child or relative until the child turns 18 or 25 years old. **Sentence:** Parents may open an *UGMA* for a child at a brokerage firm so they can invest in index funds, stocks, and mutual funds.

Unrealized gains   When a stock or other financial product moves higher (or lower if shorting) while the investor still owns the position. The term *paper gain* is also known as an unrealized gain. **Sentence:** Her *unrealized gains* of $2,000 will not be taxable until the shares are sold.

UTMA (Uniform Gifts to Minors Act)   Allows an adult to transfer real estate, fine art, and collectibles into an account on behalf of a child until the child turns 18 or 25 years old. **Sentence:** Parents may open an *UTMA* for the child which allows them to transfer fine art and other collectibles until the child is no longer a minor.

Unrealized losses   When a stock or other financial product moves lower (or higher, if shorting) but hasn't yet been sold. It's also known as a *paper loss*. **Sentence:** He has *unrealized losses* of $3,200 on a stock and cannot take a deduction on his income taxes until it is sold.

Value stocks   A stock that is trading below its true value, based on fundamentals such as earnings and dividends. **Sentence:** Value investors looking for bargains seek out *value stocks*.

Volatility/volatile   A term that describes how much a stock may change over any time period. Stocks with higher volatility undergo larger percentage price changes than a lower volatility stock. **Sentence:** The stock market is very *volatile* today, opening lower by 1%, and then closing higher by more than 2%.

Volume   The number of shares of stock traded during a certain time period, usually one day. Traders use volume to help determine whether a stock is worth buying. The higher the volume, the more interest there may be in that stock. Conversely, lower volume tells us that traders may be less interested in that stock. **Sentence:** Before buying or selling a stock, many traders check its daily *volume*.

Yield   Refers to the earnings made on an investment over a specific time period. **Sentence:** Investors, especially those who buy bonds, are very interested in the *yield*.

APPENDIX

USEFUL WEBSITES AND APPS

f you are looking for additional information, consider looking at the following websites and apps. Those organizations preceded by an asterisk (*) indicate that they are accessible through a paid subscription.

*AAII: http://www.aaii.com

Bankrate: http://www.bankrate.com

Barchart: http://www.barchart.com

*Barron's: http://www.barrons.com

Benzinga: http://www.benzinga.com

Bloomberg: http://www.bloomberg.com

Briefing: http://www.briefing.com

CNBC: http://www.cnbc.com

CNN Business: http://Money.cnn.com

Financial Times: http://www.ft.com

Forbes: http://www.forbes.com

Fox Business News: http://www.foxbusiness.com

Google Finance: http://www.google.com/finance

Investopedia: http://www.investopedia.com

Investor's Business Daily: http://www.investors.com

*Kiplinger: http://www.kiplinger.com

MarketWatch: http://www.marketwatch.com

The MoneyShow: http://www.moneyshow.com

Morningstar: http://www.morningstar.com

The Motley Fool: http://www.fool.com

MSN Money: http://www.msn.com

Nasdaq: http://www.nasdaq.com

New York Stock Exchange: http://www.nyse.com

NerdWallet: http://www.nerdwallet.com

Real Clear Markets: http://www.realclearmarkets.com

SEC: http://www.sec.gov

Seeking Alpha: http://www.seekingalpha.com

StockCharts: http://www.stockcharts.com

*The Street: http://www.thestreet.com

TradingView: http://www.tradingview.com

*Value Line: http://www.valueline.com

Wall Street Journal: http://www.wsj.com

Wikiinvest: http://www.wikiinvest.com

Yahoo Finance: http://finance.yahoo.com

*Zacks Investment Research: http://www.zacks.com

ACKNOWLEDGMENTS

To senior editor Judith Newlin at Wiley for her excellent suggestions and guidance in making this the best possible book. I can't thank her enough for working with me again on another successful book project. It could not have been completed without her help and that of many others at Wiley.

To assistant editor Delainey Henson at Wiley for taking care of all the details that helped to make this book possible, and to Susan Geraghty for her copyediting skills.

To Richard Samson at Wiley for moving the book along through production and working with me until the final version was completed.

To Violetta, my smartest student, for her never-ending support, and for giving me the idea that helped make this book possible.

To Eva. Because your wise mother used the strategies in this book, you should have a lifetime of financial security. I urge you to read the whole book when you are older and follow its advice.

To Mark Wolfinger, a superb fact-checker, content editor, and friend.

I appreciate the many writing opportunities that Jonathan Burton provided me at MarketWatch.

ACKNOWLEDGMENTS

To Peter Lynch, Warren Kaplan, and the late John Bogle for sharing their investment strategies and ideas with me.

I also want to thank the following friends and acquaintances for their continued support and encouragement: Alexandra Bengtsson, Angela Bengtsson, Karina Benzineb, Yan Benzineb, Tine Claes, Evrice Cornelius, Hazel Hall, Harvey Small, Lucie Stejskalova, and Giovanna Stephenson.

Finally, thanks to all the readers in the United States and from all over the world who took the time to buy and read my books. I really appreciate it.

ABOUT
THE AUTHOR

Michael Sincere interviewed some of the top traders and financial experts in the country to find out the lessons they had learned in the market so he could help others avoid the mistakes he had made. He wrote a book about these lessons, followed by more books, including *Understanding Options* (McGraw-Hill), *All About Market Indicators* (McGraw Hill), *Start Day Trading Now* (Adams Media), *Make Money Trading Options* (McGraw Hill), *How to Profit in the Stock Market* (McGraw Hill), and *Help Your Child Build Wealth* (Wiley).

Sincere has written numerous columns and magazine articles on investing and trading. He has also been interviewed on dozens of national radio programs and has appeared on financial news TV programs such as CNBC and ABC's "World News Now" to talk about his books. In addition to being a freelance writer and author, Sincere writes a column for MarketWatch, "Michael Sincere's Long-Term Trader."

When Sincere is not writing, he's riding one of his e-bikes, or traveling, or doing both. If you have questions or comments, write him at msincere@gmail.com. You can also visit Sincere's website and read his blog at www.michaelsincere.com.

INDEX

Note: Page references in *italics* refer to figures.

A
Abbott Labs, 95
active managers, 52, 64, 68
Adobe, 93
agents, real estate, 166–7
algorithms, 169–70, 178
allowances, investing money from, 59
Alphabet, 89
alternative investments, 9
Amazon, 24, 30, 89, 99–101, 117
American mutual funds, 53
analyzing stocks, 115–24
    fundamental analysis, 115–19
    stock snapshot page in, 123, *124*
    technical analysis, 115, 119–22
    watch list in, 122–3
annual reports, 116, 178
Apple
    dividends from, 111
    return on, 89, 90, 101–2
    in S&P 500 index, 30
    stock chart of, 120, *120*, 121
    stock price of, 134
    success of, 93, 99
appraisers, 167
apps, investment, 26–7, 197–8

ask price, 126, 132, 178–9
asset allocation
    Bogle on, 69
    defined, 179
    with robo-advisors, 158
assets, 179
automating monthly deposits, 60
average yearly return,
    on S&P 500, 3, 4, 40

B
balance sheet, 116, 179
Bankrate calculators, 40
bear markets
    buy-and-hold strategy in, 103
    buying growth stocks during, 97
    defined, 179
    index funds during, 37
    investing during, 16
    Kaplan on, 112
bear (or bearish), 179
beating the market, 67–8
becoming a millionaire, 40–1
Berkshire Hathaway, 36, 113
Bezos, Jeff, 100
bid-ask price, 123

203

IRAs (Individual
  Retirement Accounts)
  custodial Roth IRAs, 78–80
  defined, 186
  Roth IRAs, 77–8
  taxes on, 78
iShares U.S. Treasury Bond ETF, 51
iShares 20+ Year Treasury
  Bond ETF, 51

J
JCPenney, 91
Jobs, Steve, 101–2, 134
Johnson & Johnson, 95
joint brokerage account, 186

K
Kaplan, Warren, investing strategies
  of, 109–13
Kodak, 91

L
large-cap stocks, 186
Lehman Brothers, 91
lenders, for real estate, 166–7
leverage, 186–7
limit orders, 126, 132, 187
liquidity
  defined, 187
  of real estate, 164–5
  of SPDR &P 500 ETF, 45
  of US Treasury bonds, 161
load mutual funds, 53, 55, 187
long-term investment
  abandoning, 146
  Bogle on, 65–7
  defined, 187
  fundamental vs. technical analy-
    sis for, 135
Lowe's, 30, 95, 99, 107

lump-sum method, 58
Lynch, Peter, investing strategies
  of, 93, 105–9

M
margin, 23, 144, 187
margin accounts, 23
margin call, 148, 187–8
market capitalization, 30, 188
market orders, 126, 132, 188
maturity dates
  of government bonds, 51
  for Treasury bills, 162
  for Treasury bonds, 160
  for Treasury notes, 162
meltups, 169–70
Melvin Capital, 171
mental stop price, 188
Meta, 89, 93
Microsoft, 30, 89, 93, 99, 111
mid-cap stocks, 188
Middlesex Water, 95
millionaire, becoming a, 40–1
mining, 154
money, 4
  emotions about, 142
  healthy relationship with, 7
  for investing, 139
  learning to save, 6
  losing, 141–2
  making, ease of, 139
  that you make vs. that
    you keep, 160
  withdrawing, 176
money-making strategies, 57–70
  automating monthly deposits, 60
  Bogle on, 64–9
  creating emergency fund, 63
  dollar cost averaging, 57–9
  one rule for, 61–2

209

scaling
  into investments, 129–31
  out of investments, 135–6
scams
  with cryptocurrencies, 155
  by family, 149–52
  pump-and-dump, 147–9
Schwab S&P 500 Index Fund, 47
Schwab U.S. TIPS ETF, 51
Sears, 91, 93, 134
Securities and Exchange Commission
  (SEC), 191–2
security, 192
selling ETFs, 131–2
selling index funds
  avoiding, 146
  by children, 147
  situations for, 61–2
selling stocks, 131–6
  fundamental analysis strategies
    for, 133–4
  math for, 127–8
  in quarters and halves, 135–6
  shorting (short-selling), 169–71, 192
  steps in, 131–2
  technical analysis
    strategies for, 135
  timing for, 132–3, 139–41
  traps and pitfalls in (see
    psychological traps and pitfalls)
selling Treasury bonds, 160–1
shareholders, 33
shares
  buying, 24
  defined, 192
  goal of buying, 11–12
  of indexes, 30
  in mutual funds, 54
shorting (short-selling), 169–71, 192
sideways trends, 121
simulated (paper) trading, 190

small-cap stocks, 192
socially responsible investing
  (SRI), 192
S&P 500, 13, 29–31
  average yearly return on, 3, 4, 40
  Buffett on, 36
  defined, 192–3
  as diversified investment, 32–3
  index ETFs, 43–8
  index mutual funds, 47–8
  long-term wins with, 39
  main index products for, 43–4
  popularity of, 29
  professional managers' use of, 13, 14
  pros' failure to beat, 1–2
  symbol for, 24
S&P 500 Dividend Aristocrats, 95
S&P 500 Dividend Aristocrats EFT, 95
SPDR S&P Dividend ETF, 49, 111
SPDR S&P 500 ETF, 24, 45
S&P 500 index ETFs, 44–6
S&P 500 index mutual funds, 47–8
SRI (socially responsible
  investing), 192
Standard & Poor's 500 see S&P 500
stock brokerage firms, 20–2 see also
  brokerage firms
stockbrokers, in managing brokerage
  account, 21
stock chart, 119–22, 120
  defined, 193
  moving averages on, 121–2
  trends on, 120–1
  volume on, 122
stock exchange, 193
stock investing, 9
stock market, 11–17
  Bogle on drops in, 66–7
  declines or corrections in, 145
  defined, 11, 193
  described, 11–12